MW00399125

Common Grace Revisited

Rightly Dividing the Word of Truth

———— •·•·• ————

Under the series title Rightly Dividing the Word of Truth, the Reformed Free Publishing Association (RFPA) embarks on the publication of its paperback series. Based on solidly Reformed biblical exegesis and lively application of the Reformed creeds, the chapters of these volumes originally appeared as series articles in the *Standard Bearer*, the semi-monthly periodical also published by the RFPA. The goal of publishing this series is to give broader life to the subjects as originally treated by the *Standard Bearer* editorial staff. The RFPA initially intends to make two volumes available per year on a variety of timely topics.

The initial titles to be released are:

David J. Engelsma, *Common Grace Revisited*
David J. Engelsma, Barry Gritters, Charles Terpstra, *Reformed Worship*

Additional titles are under consideration.

Common Grace Revisited

A Response to Richard J. Mouw's
He Shines in All That's Fair

David J. Engelsma

Reformed Free Publishing Association
Grandville, Michigan

© 2003 Reformed Free Publishing Association
All rights reserved
Printed in the United States of America

No part of this book may by used or reprinted in any form without
permission from the publisher, except in the case of a brief quotation
used in connection with a critical article or review.

Scriptures cited by the author are taken from the
Authorized (King James) Version of the Bible

For information, contact:
Reformed Free Publishing Association
4949 Ivanrest Ave SW
Grandville, MI 49418-9709
Phone: (616) 224-1518
Fax: (616) 224-1517
Website: www.rfpa.org
E-mail: mail@rfpa.org

ISBN 0-916206-81-5
LCCN 2003093905

to Aunt Win

Contents

Contents

Contents

Preface

————◆·◆·◆————

The book on common grace by Reformed theologian and evangelical leader, Richard J. Mouw, *He Shines in All That's Fair: Culture and Common Grace*, does several worthwhile things. It indicates the great importance of common grace for the Christian life in the thinking of its defenders. It offers a candid explanation of the real reasons why men and churches embrace common grace. And it recognizes the opposition to common grace on the part of the Protestant Reformed Churches as a reasonable, even legitimate, position within the framework of Calvinism.

Mouw's book is a fresh study of the doctrine of common grace by an enthusiastic advocate. Particularly in a fascinating linking of common grace with an infralapsarian view of the decrees of God, the book breaks new ground.

The book fairly begs for a response from the opposition. Such is *Common Grace Revisited*. The response takes up Mouw's arguments, especially the appeal to the seeming good of the non-elect, the affirmation of God's "empathy" with the ungodly in both their joys and their sorrows, and the assertion of God's gracious work in culture.

But the response does more. It proposes a biblical, distinctively Reformed alternative to common grace for active Christian life in the world.

I am well aware that the immediate and overwhelming reaction of evangelicals and of Reformed Christians to Mouw's book is wholehearted approval. Mouw preaches (and preaches effectively) to the choir.

I am also aware, only too well aware, that a book opposing common grace will meet with widespread hostility. I am preaching, after a manner of speaking, to the "unconverted." But I may ask for a hearing on the important doctrine, and for a judgment on the biblical and creedal merits of the case. I ask for this hearing and for this judgment.

DAVID J. ENGELSMA
Professor of Dogmatics and Old Testament Studies
Theological School of the Protestant Reformed Churches

1

A New Look at Common Grace

———•◦•◦•———

"HE SHINES IN ALL THAT'S FAIR" IS A LOVELY LINE IN the well-known hymn, "This Is My Father's World."

> This is my Father's world: the birds their carols raise,
> The morning light, the lily white, declare their Maker's praise.
> This is my Father's world: He shines in all that's fair;
> In the rustling grass I hear Him pass;
> He speaks to me everywhere.

Dr. Richard J. Mouw has lifted this line from the hymn and made it the title of his recent book, *He Shines in All That's Fair: Culture and Common Grace.*[1] As Mouw rightly suggests, the book is important, not only for the entire Reformed community, but also for the wider circles of evangelicalism and even "segments of mainstream Protestantism": "the underlying issues here are of broad contemporary Christian concern," important for "the larger Christian theological world" (pp. 4, 3, 8).

Common Grace Revisited

He Shines in All That's Fair is a reappraisal of certain issues involved in the common grace controversy in the Christian Reformed Church in the early 1920s. The subtitle is *Culture and*

---

1. Grand Rapids, Mich.: Eerdmans, 2001.

Common Grace. The subtitle makes plain that the interest of Dr. Mouw is that aspect of common grace that consists of a non-saving love of God for the reprobate wicked in this life. In His common grace love for the non-elect, God is thought to desire their earthly good, to bless them with temporal blessings, to pity them in their earthly woes, and to give them His Holy Spirit, keeping them from being totally depraved and enabling them to perform good works in society. Common grace accounts for the seeming good in unregenerated unbelievers, about whom the Reformed faith confesses in Question and Answer 8 of the Heidelberg Catechism that they are "so far depraved that [they] are wholly unapt to any good, and prone to all evil."[2] Common grace also becomes the basis of friendship between Christian and non-Christian. Especially is common grace put forward as the basis of cooperation between believers and unbelievers in working together for a good culture.

In short, Mouw's interest in *He Shines in All That's Fair* is the doctrine of common grace adopted by the Christian Reformed Church in 1924, exclusive of the "well-meant offer of the gospel."[3] Basically, this was the theory of common grace that was taught by Abraham Kuyper and Herman Bavinck: a non-saving favor of God to all humans; an operation of the Holy Spirit within the reprobate which, without regenerating them, restrains sin in them so that they are only partially depraved; and the ability of unbelievers, by virtue of this grace of the Holy Spirit, to do good works, especially on behalf of a culture which is truly, though not ultimately, good.

"My special focus," writes Mouw, early on in the book,

---

2. Heidelberg Catechism, Q & A 8, in vol. 3 of *Creeds of Christendom,* ed. Philip Schaff (Grand Rapids, Mich.: Baker Book House, 1966), 310.

3. The three points of common grace, adopted by the Christian Reformed Church in 1924 and Herman Hoeksema's criticism of them are found in Herman Hoeksema, "A Triple Breach in the Foundation of the Reformed Truth" (Evangelism Committee of Southwest Protestant Reformed Church, Grandville, Mich., repr., 2001).

will be on the relevance of teachings about common grace for our understanding of *culture* in our contemporary context. Is there a non-saving grace that is at work in the broader reaches of human cultural interaction, a grace that expedites a desire on God's part to bestow certain blessings on all human beings, elect and non-elect alike—blessings that provide the basis for Christians to co-operate with, and learn from, non-Christians? (p. 14).

Significant Issues for the
Entire Christian Community

It is Mouw's judgment and experience that the controversy over common grace in the Christian Reformed Church was of great importance. "The issues relating to the idea of common grace and the battles that have been waged over those issues have long fascinated me. In a sense, questions about common grace have formed the underlying issues in my own intellectual pilgrimage" (p. vii).

These issues are important not only for Mouw personally. "The underlying issues here are of broad contemporary Christian concern" (p. 3). Indeed, Mouw is convinced that "much important content in these Calvinist debates has been hidden too long from the larger Christian theological world. My efforts here, then, are an attempt to give Dutch Reformed deliberations about common grace some broader ecumenical exposure" (p. 8).

The Protestant Reformed Churches are likewise convinced of the vital importance of the issues involved in their controversy with the Christian Reformed Church, and now most of the Reformed world, over common grace. We are delighted that a man of the theological stature of Richard Mouw opens up a public discussion of these issues. Mouw is a leading figure, not only in Reformed circles but also in the wider evangelical sphere. For many years, he taught philosophy at Calvin College in Grand Rapids, Michigan. At present, he is president of the huge and influential Fuller Theological Seminary in Pasadena, California.

Dr. Mouw's revisiting the common grace controversy of the early 1920s resulting in the formation of the Protestant Reformed Churches comes hard on the heels of the reexamination of that doctrinal struggle in several articles in the *Calvin Theological Journal* of April and November, 2000.[4] The Protestant Reformed Churches welcome these fresh analyses and hope for continuing discussion of the issues by these writers and by others.

Civility in Theological Discourse

Richard Mouw is a fair and honest controversialist. He is winsome in debate, practicing the civility that he preaches. Mouw treats the position on common grace of Herman Hoeksema and the Protestant Reformed Churches at length. In fact, the book is both occasioned by the historical controversy over common grace between the Christian Reformed Church and Herman Hoeksema and structured by Mouw's interaction with the rejection of common grace by Hoeksema and the Protestant Reformed Churches. *He Shines in All That's Fair* is Richard Mouw's defense and development of common grace on behalf of good culture against the rejection of common grace by Herman Hoeksema. It is amusing that what purported to be a review of the book in a recent issue of *Christian Renewal* managed to avoid mentioning the name of Herman Hoeksema while listing any number of others who are bit

---

4. John Bolt, "Common Grace and the Christian Reformed Synod of Kalamazoo (1924): A Seventy-Fifth Anniversary Retrospective," *Calvin Theological Journal* 35, no. 1 (April 2000): 7–36; Raymond A. Blacketer, "The Three Points in Most Parts Reformed: A Reexamination of the So-called Well-Meant Offer of Salvation," *Calvin Theological Journal* 35, no. 1 (April 2000): 37–65; John Bolt, "Common Grace, Theonomy, and Civic Good: The Temptations of Calvinistic Politics (Reflections on the Third Point of the Christian Reformed Church Kalamazoo Synod, 1924)," *Calvin Theological Journal* 35, no. 2 (November 2000): 205–237.

players in the book. That reviewer could review Melville's great novel without mentioning Moby Dick.[5] Mouw is respectful of the position on common grace of its great adversary, Herman Hoeksema. Mouw admits that common grace is difficult to grasp and describe. Like old Foppe Ten Hoor, Mouw himself is "not very clear about what it is" (p. 13). Mouw freely acknowledges that rejection of common grace would seem to follow from the Calvinist doctrines of predestination and the antithesis. In fact, Mouw puzzles over the passion with which defenders of common grace opposed Hoeksema.

In this connection, Mouw deplores the tactic of the defenders of common grace of smearing Hoeksema with the epithet "Anabaptist," as though Hoeksema's rejection of common grace amounted to "world flight." This was an extremely effective tactic at the time of the controversy, and one that is still effectively used against the Protestant Reformed Churches by the impassioned defenders of common grace.

Mouw quotes approvingly from a letter that Prof. William Heyns of the Christian Reformed seminary sent to Rev. J. K. Van Baalen, the most energetic practitioner of the tactic, chiding Van Baalen for calling Hoeksema and his colleagues Anabaptists. This is the first time, to my knowledge, that this letter has surfaced in the literature of the controversy in the Christian Reformed Church over common grace. Heretofore, William Heyns has not received good press in the Protestant Reformed Churches. Heyns is regarded as the father of the conditional covenant in the Christian Reformed Church and, thus, indirectly, of the "well-meant offer." Because of his reprimand of Van Baalen in the heat of the battle in the letter from which Mouw quotes, Heyns rises in my estimation. Contending that it was, and is, unfair to label Hoeksema an Anabaptist for his rejection of common grace, Mouw writes:

---

5. "Mouw on Common Grace," *Christian Renewal* 20, no. 9 (January 28, 2002): 7, 8.

Calvin Seminary professor William Heyns made a similar point...
in a 1922 letter to Christian Reformed minister J. K. Van Baalen,
who had just written a rather inflammatory pamphlet depicting
Hoeksema and his associates as Anabaptists. Heyns endorsed the
general thrust of Van Baalen's critique, but he chided him for his
rhetoric, instructing Van Baalen that he "would have done better
to leave out that epithet 'Anabaptist,' which here can serve only
as a scornful word." Surely, Heyns wrote, Van Baalen was not ig-
norant of the fact "that all of the same things" he found in Hoeksema's thinking could "also be said of the old theologians of
Reformed scholasticism" (p. 23).

Mouw does justice to Hoeksema's spiritual, practical concern in the controversy over common grace.

> At the heart of Herman Hoeksema's sustained critique of com-
> mon grace theology lies a very practical concern about the life of
> the church. The commonality emphasis in common grace theol-
> ogy, Hoeksema insists, will inevitably result in the "obliteration of
> the distinction between the Church and the world, light and
> darkness, Christ and Belial, righteousness and unrighteousness."
> Of course, no common grace defender would simply advocate
> the "obliteration" of the distinctions listed by Hoeksema. But it
> does seem to be essential to common grace thinking that the dis-
> tinction between "church and world" is not exactly the same dis-
> tinction as that which holds between "light and darkness, Christ
> and Belial, righteousness and unrighteousness" (p. 24).

Mouw even calls attention to the judgment of the present
editor of the *Standard Bearer* upon the worldview of common
grace, that "the worldview of common grace has proved to be
a colossal failure."[6] Although Mouw thinks that there is another, more favorable judgment that can and should be
made, he agrees that

---

6. David J. Engelsma, "The Reformed Worldview: 3. The Failure of
Common Grace (cont.)," *Standard Bearer* 74, no. 20 (September 1, 1998):
462.

he [the editor of the *Standard Bearer*] is right to insist that we take an honest look at the failure of common grace thought to stem the tide of wickedness so obvious in places like the Netherlands and North America. If we are to judge common grace teachings by looking for fruits of righteousness in the larger culture— surely a fair test, given the triumphalist tones in which these teachings have often been proclaimed—then we must admit to some serious shortcomings (p. 27).

Mouw points out, correctly, that occasionally Calvin refers to certain natural abilities in the unregenerate as a "peculiar grace" of God. Nevertheless, on the basis of Calvin's overall doctrine concerning the total depravity of the ungodly, a depravity that "sullies" all their "virtues" and renders them "worthless," Mouw concludes that opponents of common grace teachings "can legitimately claim nonetheless to be working within the general contours of Calvin's thought" (pp. 17, 18).

A More Aggressive Practice of Common Grace

On his part, however, Dr. Mouw comes down firmly on the side of common grace. Although Mouw holds the doctrine of predestination set forth in the Canons of Dordt, he believes that God has a non-saving love for all humans. In this love, He blesses all humans with many gifts, including a gracious work of the Holy Spirit within them that restrains their depravity and produces a certain goodness in them and in their works. Richard Mouw sees much in the life of many ungodly people that is fair. All this goodness, truth, and beauty is the shining of God Himself in the lives of the ungodly in His common grace. "He shines in all that's fair." This shining of God in His common grace is the basis of legitimate friendship between believer and unbeliever, as it is the basis of cooperation between believer and unbeliever to work for a good culture.

In fact, Mouw faults the three points of common grace adopted by the Christian Reformed Church in 1924 for their passivity. Mouw calls Christians aggressively to act upon and implement common grace by promoting friendships with the ungodly and cooperative cultural endeavor.

> The Christian Reformed Church's Three Points of 1924 certainly seem designed to encourage cultural passivity. They come across as instructions for Christians who are mere observers of the larger world. Of course, we cannot help being largely passive when it comes to the "natural blessings"—such as sunshine and rain—that are bestowed upon the elect and non-elect alike. But the second and third areas are different. We should not just stand back and watch for signs that God is restraining sin in the world, or hope that we might witness acts of civic righteousness popping up here and there in the lives of the unredeemed. We ought to look for ways God can use us to restrain the power of sin in the larger human community, and to perform our own works of civic good (pp. 80, 81).

Dr. Mouw's reasons for espousing common grace are characteristically candid. They are also interesting. We will look at them in the next chapter.

2

The Real Reasons for Common Grace

———•·•·•———

As the previous chapter pointed out, *He Shines in All That's Fair: Culture and Common Grace* contends that the theory of common grace adopted by the Christian Reformed Church in 1924 can be helpful to all Christians. Its usefulness is that, in a world of division and strife, it provides a basis for the friendship of Christian and non-Christian and, especially, for the cooperation of Christians with non-Christians in working for a decent, humane, and even God-glorifying culture.

With the notable exception of its teaching of a "well-meant offer of salvation" to all who hear the gospel, which was added by the Christian Reformed Church,[1] the theory of common grace that the Christian Reformed Church adopted in 1924 is basically the doctrine that was developed by the Dutch Reformed theologians Abraham Kuyper and Herman Bavinck. The theory holds that God has an attitude of favor in history toward all humans without exception. In this common favor, God gives to all, the reprobate ungodly as well as the elect believers, such material gifts as health and family, rain and sunshine, and wealth and long life. In this favor, He also works in all men by His Holy Spirit. To this gracious operation of the Spirit in the unregenerated are due

---

1. For a thorough treatment of that aspect of common grace that consists of the "well-meant offer of the gospel," see David J. Engelsma, *Hyper-Calvinism and the Call of the Gospel*. Revised 2nd ed. (Grand Rapids, Mich.: Reformed Free Publishing Association, 1994).

both his natural gifts, for example, the musical ability of a Mozart and the putting prowess of a Tiger Woods, and, more importantly, the restraint of sin in him so that he is only partially depraved.

By virtue of the good that is in him by the gracious, though non-saving, operation of the Spirit, the unregenerated can perform works that are truly good. This goodness of the non-Christian is the ground of the Christian's friendship with him, of the Christian's appreciation of much of the culture of the ungodly world, and of the Christian's cooperation with unbelievers to develop a culture that is even better.

Dr. Mouw urges a more active use of common grace by those Calvinists who confess it. He is critical of the passivity of many, who seem to be content merely to recognize common grace in the falling of the rain on the wicked and in the good deeds of unbelievers. Calvinists who confess common grace must proclaim it as a basis of the shared life of all humanity and as a foundation of united cultural endeavor. These Calvinists must also aggressively practice common grace in "common grace ministries," for example, teaching in the public schools, counseling non-Christians with psychological and marital problems, helping the poor, and addressing national policies and problems in the "public square."

Mouw himself emphasizes the "empathy" of God that is implied by common grace. In His favor to all, God shares the feelings of unbelieving men and women. God rejoices with the non-Christian husband and wife who are reconciled after the husband's adultery. He sympathizes with the Muslim mother whose child is brutally murdered before her eyes by her oppressors.

Even though he is an advocate of common grace, Richard Mouw takes seriously the opposition to the theory of common grace by Herman Hoeksema and the Protestant Reformed Churches. The arguments of Dr. Mouw in defense of common grace, against the objections of Hoeksema and the Protestant Reformed Churches, are the concern of this chapter.

Absence of Scripture

Scripture plays almost no role whatever in Mouw's apology for common grace. There is a reference to Revelation 21:24–26 as the passage that Abraham Kuyper and Herman Bavinck explained as teaching that "the glory and honor of pagan cultures" will enter into the holy city in the Day of Christ. But this passage says nothing about a grace of God toward pagans. Verse 27 warns that nothing will enter the holy Jerusalem "that defileth, neither whatsoever worketh abomination, or maketh a lie."

The notion of Kuyper and Bavinck is absurd. Will the angels carry into heaven a copy of Plato's *Symposium*? Michelangelo's *David*? Leonardo's *The Last Supper*? The score of Beethoven's *Symphony No. 9*? Mouw himself is rightly dubious of the enthusiastic endorsement of heathen culture by the two Dutch theologians: "Those of us who endorse the idea of common grace would do well to recognize the ways in which its teachings frequently have fostered a triumphalist spirit that has encouraged false hopes for a premature transformation of sinful culture" (p. 50).

Mouw's appeal to 1 Peter 2:11–17, the related exhortation in 1 Peter 3:15, 16, and a corresponding passage in the Old Testament, Jeremiah 29, is not intended to prove a grace of God at work among the heathen and ungodly, but a certain calling of the people of God toward the heathen and ungodly (pp. 76–78).

Only in the last chapter, late in the development of his defense of common grace, does Dr. Mouw bring up Luke 6:35, a text that is important in the controversy over common grace. Even then, Mouw's use of the text is cautious and limited. He appeals to it against Hoeksema's assertion that God "hates His enemies and purposes to destroy them, except them He chose in Christ Jesus." Hoeksema's assertion, says Mouw, "does not seem to comport well, however, with Christ's command to 'love your enemies, and do good, expecting nothing in return' even as the Father 'is kind to the ungrateful and the wicked' (Luke 6:35)." Then, overlooking that Hoeksema had denied that *God* loves *His* reprobate enemies, not that *we* should love *our* unbelieving enemies, Mouw adds, "When the Savior refers here to people who curse us and abuse us, is he thinking exclusively of our *Christian* enemies? It seems unlikely" (p. 83).

This is the extent of the reference to, and use of, Scripture. One text bearing on the issue of common grace is quoted in part and is then very briefly and hesitantly explained as favoring a grace of God to the reprobate ungodly.

This is not intended as a criticism of Dr. Mouw. There can be no doubt whatever that he knows all the passages that the defenders of common grace have adduced in support of the doctrine. We may be sure that he is thoroughly conversant as well with the interpretation of these texts by the defenders of common grace. But Richard Mouw is a candid man. The real reason why he embraces and promotes common grace is not the clear, compelling testimony of Holy Scripture. He says as much when he admits that, after forty years of studying the issue, he is still not clear as to what common grace is.

Real Reasons for Common Grace

In *He Shines in All That's Fair*, Richard Mouw sets forth the real reasons for his acceptance and advocacy of a common grace of God. Mouw, a Christian and a Reformed man, sees in unregenerated men and women in southern California and elsewhere a goodness that does not harmonize with the Reformed doctrine of total depravity. He sees non-Christians who are decent, moral, friendly, loving, kind, and compassionate. He sees men and women who are avowed unbelievers performing works that are good: reconciling in marriage, caring for their children, helping the poor, giving their life in selfless devotion to their country or their fellowmen.

The reason for Mouw's advocacy of common grace is that he finds in himself an empathy with ungodly people that seems to conflict with the Reformed faith's teaching that God hates the reprobate wicked. Mouw takes delight in the putting ability of a Sabbath–desecrating professional golfer. Much more important to the Fuller Seminary theologian is his pity for the Muslim mother, worshiper of Allah, whose infant child is killed before her eyes by the men who have just raped her.

And the reason for his embrace of common grace is that Dr. Richard Mouw, learned, influential Christian scholar and teacher, thinks that he and other Christians should be able to cooperate with unbelievers on behalf of a culture of justice, mercy, and peace. But he is well aware of the Reformed doctrine of the antithesis between the church and the world, believer and unbeliever, godly and ungodly. *He Shines in All That's Fair* has a lengthy section on the antithesis (pp. 14–29). Mouw is not of a mind to repudiate the antithesis. On the contrary, he takes issue with his mentor, Henry Stob, who was inclined to limit the antithesis to opposing principles of goodness and evil in the world. Mouw recognizes that the biblical antithesis comes between persons.

A theory that accounts for what Mouw sees, feels, and thinks is common grace. Does he see goodness in the world of fallen men and women? A common grace of God must be at work in this world. Does he feel pity for the tormented Muslim woman? This pity must be a reflection of a common grace compassion that God Himself has for the woman, idolater though she is. Does he desire to work together with non-Christians to hold together the fragmenting culture of North America and even to make it a good culture? This desire must be grounded ultimately in a purpose of God Himself to create good, "godly" cultures in history by the common grace efforts of decent unbelievers and especially by the united efforts of believers and unbelievers.

Common grace solves the problem of the discrepancy between what Mouw sees, feels, and thinks, and what the Reformed confession maintains. Mouw sees goodness in the world of fallen, natural men and women, whereas the Reformed confession teaches total depravity. The solution is a common grace of God that gives some deliverance from the condition of total depravity without affirming the natural goodness of fallen man.

Mouw's pity for an idolater suggests a compassion of God for the reprobate wicked, whereas the Reformed confession teaches that God is compassionate toward the elect only and that His wrath is revealed from heaven against the pagans who hold the truth under in unrighteousness. The solution is a common grace favor of God toward the wicked, distinct from His special, saving grace to the elect.

Mouw thinks that he should form friendships with non-Christians and that he should work with them to create a good culture, whereas the Reformed confession teaches separation and hostility between the believer and the unbeliever. The solution is a common grace of God that believer and unbeliever share and practice in the sphere of everyday, earthly life, while remaining separated in worship and salvation.

Common grace is the distinctly (not *distinctively*) Reformed way of accommodating the Bible's severe judgment upon the world of the ungodly and the Bible's equally stringent call to believers to spiritual separation from this world to the seemingly contrary facts of our experience. Reformed people are not the only ones to have noticed the apparent good of the ungodly, or to have felt that God ought to have some sympathy for His reprobate enemies, or to have thought it proper for Christians to enjoy friendship with non-Christians and to cooperate with non-Christians in building a good society.

Theological liberals explain these things in terms of the natural goodness and brotherhood of all mankind. Roman Catholics fall back on natural theology. These doctrines have been objectionable to Reformed theologians, although Rome's natural theology is now finding some favor. But common grace provides the very same conclusions and warrants the very same practices as liberalism and Roman Catholicism: the goodness of unregenerated man; a love of God for all; the friendship (brotherhood?) of believer and unbeliever; and the union of church and world in building a good culture or, shall we say, a kingdom of man. And the theory of common grace has the advantage of a Reformed reputation.

In basing the theory of common grace upon his own seeing, feeling, and thinking, rather than upon the Word of God, Dr. Mouw is not unique. What sets him apart from many other defenders of common grace is his candor in acknowledging what the real basis of common grace is. Common grace as developed by Kuyper and Bavinck, adopted by the Christian Reformed Church in 1924, and now widely advertised in the Reformed community as one of the hallmarks of Calvinism is simply not the doctrinal fruit of careful, thorough study of the Word of God. Scripture does not teach the partial depravity of the unregenerated. Scripture does not teach that the works of those who are dead in trespasses and sin are good—*good in God's judgment as the product of His grace*. Scripture does not share the enthusiasm of the defenders of common grace for the possibilities of a good culture as the result of the united efforts of the church and the world. It is extremely difficult to find Scripture permitting, much less commanding, the friendship of the seed of the woman with the seed of the serpent.

The theory of common grace that is now a shibboleth in Reformed churches does not derive from John Calvin. Calvin on the rare occasion speaks unadvisedly of a "peculiar grace" in the ungodly, usually in connection with Calvin's recognition of outstanding natural gifts possessed by them. But one will search Calvin in vain for a grace that renders the unbeliever only partially depraved, that produces a positively good culture from the efforts of those who hate God, that is a basis of the friendship of Christian and non-Christian, and that expresses the purpose of God to create good cultures in history apart from His crucified and risen Son. The father of culture-building common grace in the Reformed tradition is not John Calvin, but Abraham Kuyper. Common grace is certainly not a main theme in the theology of John Calvin. It is not even a theme. It is barely mentioned.

Doing Theology at Monroe and Division

Common grace is based on what men see, feel, and think as they observe their neighbors and the world. This explains its popularity and its endurance, in spite of the contrary testimony of the Reformed confessions and in spite of its lack of support in the Bible. The thinking of the defenders of common grace is, "Let the critics of common grace say what they will, we see good in the ungodly; we feel pity for them in their woe, and God should feel pity also; we cannot help but think that we ought to pitch in with the decent non-Christians to make our society, and man's life in it, good—a society reflecting, not Christ, but 'Judeo-Christian principles.' "

If the issue is to be decided on the basis of what men see, feel, and think, the theory of common grace wins hands down. For we critics of common grace also see fine, decent, moral, friendly, likable unbelievers. We too see good in the ungodly—much good. Sympathizing with the suffering neighbor who worships another god, or no god at all, we too wonder why God does not feel pity for him. We also groan over the division, folly, injustice, and misery of human life in society, in our nation, and in the world and are tempted to suppose that the Christian is permitted, indeed called, to join with non-Christians in what would then seem the noblest of all causes: creating a society, a nation, a world, of justice, peace, beauty, and goodness.

Without the gospel and Spirit of Jesus Christ!

We see such things, feel such things, and think such things when we see, feel, and think apart from the Word of God.

This was what Herman Hoeksema was warning against, I now realize, when more than once during my seminary days he said, "Do not do your theology on the corner of Monroe and Division" (in those days, the heart of the life of the city of Grand Rapids).

Neither may Richard Mouw do his theology on the streets of southern California. Regardless of the seemingly contrary evidence of our experience of the world, we must resolutely form our theology from Holy Scripture, guided by the Reformed confessions.

Then it will be true that "He shines in all that's fair," but the "fair" must be truly "fair." And it will also be true, and our theology will state, that He curses all that's foul.

3

One Text

———•·•·•———

Even though the reasons for Dr. Mouw's embrace of common grace are his perception of good in the world of the ungodly, his feelings of delight and pity regarding the abilities and the woes of the wicked, and his conviction that believers must cooperate with unbelievers in the building of a good culture, he does appeal to one biblical text in support of his belief. He also refers to two significant passages in the Reformed confessions. Before we consider his arguments from the apparent good of the ungodly, from the Christian's pity for the distressed idolater, and from the involvement of believers in culture, we must look at Mouw's biblical and confessional proof for common grace.

A Prominent Text in the Common Grace Controversy

The one Scripture text that Mouw adduces in support of common grace is Luke 6:35. This is a text that has played a prominent role in the controversy over common grace in Reformed circles. Defenders of common grace have always appealed to it as one of the clearest, most powerful proofs of a favor of God to the reprobate wicked. The text reads: "But love ye your enemies, and do good, and lend, hoping for nothing again; and your reward shall be great, and ye shall be the children of the Highest: for he is kind unto the unthankful and

18

to the evil." The text is part of the passage beginning with verse 27 in which Jesus calls His disciples to love their enemies.

Dr. Mouw interprets the text as teaching that "God has a positive, albeit non-salvific, regard for those who are not elect, a regard that he asks us to cultivate in our own souls" (p. 82). Mouw thinks that the "unthankful and ... evil" to whom God is kind are all humans without exception, particularly those men and women whom God has eternally reprobated (p. 83).

Dr. Mouw is certainly right when he insists that the text requires believers to love their unbelieving enemies. For all we know, they may be reprobates. They hate us, curse us, and persecute us. They are our enemies on account of our confession of Christ. They need our prayers, that they be converted and saved.

I hope that Dr. Mouw does not suppose that as part of their opposition to common grace Protestant Reformed people deny that they are to love their unbelieving neighbors. He leaves the impression of this misunderstanding. Having quoted Herman Hoeksema to the effect that *God* hates *His* reprobate enemies, Mouw appeals to Luke 6:35 as teaching that *we* must love *our* unbelieving enemies (p. 83). That we must love our neighbor, whether Christian or non-Christian, is not the issue. The question is: Does God love His reprobate enemies? Specifically, the question is: Are the unthankful and evil who are the objects of God's kindness in Luke 6:35 *reprobate* persons?

Defenders of common grace assume that the unthankful and evil who are the objects of God's kindness in Luke 6:35 are all men without exception, thus including those whom He reprobated. Assuming this, they do not bother carefully to explain the last part of Luke 6:35 in the light of its context. It is enough that they cite it. But this begs the question. All agree that God is kind to unthankful and evil people. What needs to be proved is that God is kind to *all* humans who are unthankful and evil. More specifically, what needs to be proved is that God is kind to unthankful and evil *reprobates*.

What Manner of Kindness?

Plainly, Luke 6:35 cannot bear the interpretation given it by the defenders of common grace. This interpretation is that God is kind to reprobate unthankful and evil men with a non-saving, common grace kindness. As Dr. Mouw puts it, God's kindness in Luke 6:35 is a "positive, albeit non-salvific, regard for those who are not elect" (p. 82). But the text teaches the *saving* grace, or kindness, of God toward unthankful and evil people. The word that is translated "kind" is the Greek word *chreestos*. This word is used of God elsewhere in the New Testament in 1 Peter 2:3 and in Romans 2:4. In 1 Peter 2:3, where the King James Version translates the word as "gracious," the word refers to God's kindness in saving His elect. "As newborn babes," regenerated believers are to desire the sincere milk of the Word, "if so be ye have tasted that the Lord is *gracious*" (*chreestos*). In Romans 2:4, the King James Version translates *chreestos* as "goodness": "Or despisest thou the riches of his goodness and forbearance and longsuffering; not knowing that the *goodness* of God leadeth thee to repentance?" Inasmuch as this goodness, or kindness, of God leads one to repentance, it is a *saving* kindness, not a common grace kindness.

The use of the same word to describe the attitude of the saints likewise shows kindness to be a saving perfection. Ephesians 4:32 exhorts church members to be "*kind* one to another, tenderhearted, forgiving one another, even as God for Christ's sake hath forgiven you." The expression of kindness is forgiveness of sins.

If the unthankful and evil in Luke 6:35 are reprobate men and women, the text teaches that God is kind to them with a *saving* kindness, or grace. He saves these unthankful and evil people, leading them to repentance and forgiving their sins.

That the kindness of verse 35 is saving grace, not a common grace kindness, is established by verse 36: "Be ye therefore merciful, as your Father also is merciful." In the love and kindness that we must show to our enemies, we are to be merciful. Our mercy reflects the mercy of our Father. Although the objects of our Father's mercy are not explicitly stated in verse 36, there can be no doubt that they are the same unthankful and evil persons who are mentioned in verse 35. God is merciful to the same persons to whom He is kind, and His mercy is the supreme manifestation of His kindness. But the divine mercy is a pity of God toward sinners that yearns to deliver them from their sins and from the misery of their sins. Mercy is not a mere desire to give a wretched sinner some rain on his corn field, or a pork chop on his plate, or even a happy marriage.

If the unthankful and evil of Luke 6:35 are all humans without exception, including especially the reprobate, the text teaches far too much for the defenders of common grace. It does not teach a meager "positive, albeit non-salvific, regard for those who are not elect." It teaches a robust kindness that wills to save them. It teaches a pity toward them that yearns to redeem them.

This understanding of the kindness of God in Luke 6:35 is demanded by the preceding context, verses 27 and following. There is a relation between our love for our neighbors and God's love for the unthankful and evil. Our love reflects His love: "Be ye therefore merciful, *as* your Father also is merciful" (v. 36). Like Father, like children: "But love ye your enemies... *and ye shall be the children of the Highest*" (v. 35). In our love for our enemies, we are to pray for them, that is, pray for their salvation: "Pray for them which despitefully use you" (v. 28). This implies a sincere desire on our part for their repentance and salvation. If now the kindness of God that we reflect is a kindness toward all without exception, including reprobate men and women, God too must sincerely desire the repentance and salvation of all without exception. But such a kindness, or grace, is not common grace, a "non-salvific regard for those who are not elect." It is saving grace.

Who Are the Unthankful and Evil?

Scripture denies that God is kind and merciful to unthankful and evil reprobates, having compassion on them in their misery, willing their salvation, leading them to repentance, and forgiving their sins: "For he saith to Moses, I will have mercy on whom I will have mercy, and I will have compassion on whom I will have compassion . . . Therefore hath he mercy on whom he will have mercy, and whom he will he hardeneth" (Rom. 9:15, 18). Scripture teaches that the Christ of God, carrying out the will of God who sent Him, refused to pray for all men without exception. Thus, He showed that He did not sincerely desire the salvation of all without exception. He prayed only for those whom the Father had given Him out of the world. "I pray for them: I pray not for the world, but for them which thou hast given me; for they are thine" (John 17:9).

The meaning of Luke 6:35 is that we Christians are to love our neighbors, including our enemies. These enemies are unbelievers, non-Christians, who are hostile toward us because of our confession and discipleship of Christ. They may well be reprobate enemies, although we hope that our prayers and kind behavior may be useful to win them to Christ.

In loving our enemies, we reflect the character of our Father. Like Father, like children. For God is kind to unthankful and evil people. He is not kind to *all* unthankful and evil people. Nor does Luke 6:35 say this. But He is kind to people who are unthankful and evil. These are the elect in Christ, "the children of the Highest," who now are called and privileged to show the marvelous goodness of their heavenly Father in their own attitude and behavior toward their enemies.

We were the unthankful and evil when in kindness He set His love upon us in the eternal decree of election.

We were the unthankful and evil when in kindness He gave up His own Son for us in the redeeming death of the cross.

We were the unthankful and evil when in kindness He translated us by the regenerating Spirit into the kingdom of His dear Son.

And still we are the unthankful and evil when daily, in kindness, He brings us to repentance, forgives our sins, preserves us in the faith, and shows us a fatherly face in Jesus Christ. For, although by His grace we are also thankful and holy, we have only a very small beginning of this thankfulness and holiness. How unthankful we are for the love of God to us in Jesus Christ! And this is evil! This is a great evil!

He Shines in All That's Fair appeals to one text in support of common grace: Luke 6:35. But this text does not teach a common grace of God. It teaches a saving kindness of God. If the unthankful and evil in the text are all humans without exception, the text teaches that the saving grace of God is universal, a doctrine that the rest of Scripture denies, a doctrine that the Reformed confessions condemn, and a doctrine that Dr. Mouw repudiates.

Since this is a text that all defenders of common grace thoughtlessly appeal to, it may be hoped that others as well will now reconsider their use of it in defense of common grace and, perhaps, their defense of common grace itself.

A Particular "Common Grace"

I idly wonder whether the defenders of common grace ever recognize that their interpretation of Luke 6:35 fails even on the assumptions of the theory of common grace. Suppose that the kindness of the text is a common grace kindness of God. In this imaginary case, God's kindness is His loving desire to give everybody a comfortable physical life, nice material things, and earthly happiness, as well as His actual bestowal of all this upon everybody.

But God is not kind in this way to all unthankful and evil people. What about the millions of children born into poverty, famine, sickness, and abuse? What about the hundreds of thousands born with dreadful handicaps of body and mind? What about the millions wracked with pain, crushed with burdens, broken with disappointments, desolate with despair, terrified by fears, and destroyed by war?

Is God kind with a common grace kindness to all un-

thankful and evil people? Is He thus kind even to most unthankful and evil people?

I do not see it.

His supposed common grace proves to be as particular as
His (real) saving grace.

4

Common Grace in the Creeds?

————•∙•∙•————

FOR REFORMED AND PRESBYTERIAN DEFENDERS OF common grace, it has always been a huge embarrassment that the confessions do not teach common grace. The total absence from the Reformation creeds of a doctrine of common grace is especially a problem in view of the importance that these Reformed and Presbyterian theologians and churches attribute to common grace. With reference to the Old Testament temple, one Christian Reformed zealot called common grace one of the two pillars of the Reformed faith. Although contemporary defenders of common grace are not so picturesque in their praise of it, they too regard common grace as a prominent, even fundamental, doctrine of the Reformed, Christian faith.

Common grace largely accounts for the development of the human race and its culture. Common grace largely determines the relations of believers and unbelievers and of the church and the world. Common grace powers the Christian's involvement in everyday, earthly life in society.

Such a gracious work of God in history, in the human race, and even in the lives of Christians is no inconsiderable matter.

Why are the Reformed and Presbyterian creeds perfectly silent about this important matter? Why do neither the Three Forms of Unity nor the Westminster Standards breathe a word about this pillar in the New Testament temple of God?

It is not merely the case that the confessions are silent about a common grace of God. In certain of the doctrines that most distinguish the Reformed confessions, these confessions evidently reject and condemn the theory of common grace. Common grace teaches the partial depravity of the unregenerated; the confessions teach the total depravity of the unregenerated.[1] Common grace teaches that some works of the unregenerate are good; the confessions teach that all the works of the unregenerate are sinful.[2] Common grace teaches that God has a favor toward all men without exception; the confessions teach that "the wrath of God abideth upon those who believe not this gospel."[3] The very notion that grace is *common* contradicts the teaching that is central in the confessions: the particularity of grace.[4]

The Protestant Reformed Churches outside the Camp

It is exceedingly strange, therefore, that Reformed and Presbyterian churches and theologians put the Protestant Reformed Churches outside the camp because of these churches' rejection of common grace. The Christian Reformed Church did this in actual fact by ecclesiastical discipline in 1924/1925. The Reformed and Presbyterian community is still doing this in effect today.

This came home to me again recently. Reviewing a book by a Protestant Reformed author (never mind that it was mine), the minister of a reputedly conservative Presbyterian church in Scotland told his readers, "I do not feel that this book could be recommended." Why not? "This book is written by a minister of the Protestant Reformed Churches in America... Two of the distinctives of this church are a denial of Common Grace and a high view of baptism."[5]

---

1. Heidelberg Catechism, Q & A 8, in *Creeds of Christendom,* 310.

2. Westminster Confession of Faith, 16.7, in *Creeds of Christendom,* 635, 636.

3. Canons of Dordt, I, 4, in *Creeds of Christendom,* 581.

4. Canons of Dordt, I; Westminster Confession of Faith, 3, in *Creeds of Christendom,* 581; 608.

5. "Book Reviews," *Free Church Witness* (March 2002): 16, 17.

One cannot imagine that a "high view of baptism" disqualifies a book from being recommended to Presbyterians in Scotland by a Presbyterian magazine. But the book's rejection of "Common Grace" is the reason. Regardless that the creeds, which after all determine what is Reformed and Presbyterian, say nary a word on behalf of common grace, denial of common grace puts the Protestant Reformed Churches, their writers, and their works beyond the pale.

This is puzzling.

To his credit, Dr. Mouw calls into question this knee-jerk rejection of the Protestant Reformed Churches by the defenders of common grace: "The passion with which many of the defenders of common grace have rejected the views of Hoeksema and other critics of their position is on the face of it somewhat puzzling" (p. 20). Mouw endorses Reformed theologian Henry Van Til's hesitancy to call common grace (which Van Til embraced and promoted in a big book) *grace:*

> Henry Van Til raises the important question of whether common grace is indeed "grace" in any straightforward sense of the word. He decides that it is best "to place the term 'common grace' in quotation marks," because it seems a little odd to equate what he considers to be the very real "beneficent goodness of God to the non-elect sinners" with the redemptive "blessings which God bestows upon elect sinners in and through Jesus Christ, the Mediator." *Van Til is right to raise this caution* (p. 48; emphasis added).

Common Grace in the Canons

Despite this caution, Dr. Mouw thinks to find the teaching of common grace in two places in the Reformed confessions. These articles of the creeds are not the real reason for his belief of common grace, as I showed earlier. But we who, like Dr. Mouw, take the confessions seriously as the authoritative definition of Reformed Christianity must consider his appeal to the confessions. His first reference is to the phrase "saving good," in the Canons of Dordt:

> Therefore all men are conceived in sin, and are by nature chil-
> dren of wrath, incapable of any saving good, prone to evil, dead
> in sin, and in bondage thereto; and, without the regenerating
> grace of the Holy Spirit, they are neither able nor willing to re-
> turn to God, to reform the depravity of their nature, nor to dis-
> pose themselves to reformation.[6]

Mouw supposes that the mention of "*saving* good" implies
the existence of a non-saving good, which the natural man is
able to perform by virtue of a common grace of God. Mouw
writes concerning his understanding of the phrase "saving
good" in the Canons:

> While the Heidelberg Catechism makes the unqualified judg-
> ment that apart from the regenerating grace of God we are in-
> capable of "*any* good," the Canons of Dort introduce an
> appropriate nuance, telling us that we are all "by nature children
> of wrath, incapable of any *saving* good"—thus leaving open the
> possibility of deeds that are morally laudable without meriting sal-
> vation (p. 38).

From the Canons' denial that the unregenerated man can
do *saving* good, Mouw infers that the Canons allow for an ability of the unregenerated man to do *non-saving* good. Even if
this inference is sound, it proves absolutely nothing for a common grace of God. Neither this article of the Canons nor any
other article attributes this supposed ability of the natural
man to do non-saving good to any grace of God in him. If the
Canons do indeed imply that the natural man is still capable
of doing non-saving good, the explanation must be simply
that fallen man remains human, retaining "glimmerings of
natural light," by virtue of creation and providence, as the
next article of the Canons will teach. To introduce grace as
the explanation is completely unwarranted, both as regards
the article itself and as regards the whole of the Canons. Creation and providence are one thing; grace is quite another.

---

6. Canons of Dordt, III/IV, 3, in *Creeds of Christendom*, 588.

But Dr. Mouw's inference is mistaken. If the phrase in question were all that the Canons said about the ability for good of the unregenerated man, the inference might be allowed. But the Canons say more than only the phrase "incapable of any saving good." And what they say more is an explicit denial of Dr. Mouw's inference. His inference is that all men by nature are capable of performing deeds that, although not the fruit of the saving work of the Spirit of Christ and done outside the sphere of salvation, are yet good. These would be the works of the unbeliever that show regard for virtue, good order in society, and maintaining an orderly external deportment.

Exactly about these works of the unregenerated, the immediately following article of the Canons states:

> But so far is this light of nature from being sufficient to bring him [unregenerated man] to a saving knowledge of God, and to true conversion, that he is incapable of using it aright even in things natural and civil. Nay farther, this light, such as it is, man in various ways renders wholly polluted, and holds it [back] in unrighteousness; by doing which he becomes inexcusable before God.[7]

Those deeds of the natural man that impress the defenders of common grace—deeds that show regard for virtue, deeds that bring about good order in society, deeds of orderly external deportment—are not "non-saving good." Even the life and deeds of the unregenerated man in the sphere of the "natural and civil," supposedly the terrain of a common grace goodness, are unrighteous and "wholly polluted." These deeds are not pleasing to God. They do not give evidence of a favor of God upon the natural man. Rather, "by doing [them] he becomes inexcusable before God."

The reason why the natural man is incapable of "non-saving good," as he is incapable of saving good, the Canons give in the words that follow the phrase, "incapable of any saving good": "prone to evil, dead in sin, and in bondage thereto."[8]

---

7. Canons of Dordt, III/IV, 4, in *Creeds of Christendom,* 588.
8. Canons of Dordt, III/IV, 3, in *Creeds of Christendom,* 588.

One who is dead in sin is incapable of any good, "non-saving" as well as saving. One who is a slave to sin—a *slave*—can do nothing, absolutely nothing, except sin.

Common Grace in the Westminster Confession

The second reference by Dr. Mouw to the Reformed confessions on behalf of common grace is even less convincing than the appeal to the Canons. Dr. Mouw appeals to a passage in the Westminster Confession of Faith that speaks of the works done by unregenerate men:

> Works done by unregenerate men, although for the matter of them they may be things which God commands, and of good use both to themselves and others; yet because they proceed not from a heart purified by faith, nor are done in a right manner, according to the Word, nor to a right end, the glory of God; they are therefore sinful, and can not please God, or make a man meet to receive grace from God. And yet their neglect of them is more sinful and displeasing unto God.[9]

Mouw thinks that this implies that some works of the unregenerated are pleasing to God and thus good.

> In spite of the decidedly negative tone of these comments, the Westminster divines are actually making room for a measure of divine approval regarding deeds performed by the unregenerate that nonetheless conform to God's revealed standards. Since the "*neglect* of [such deeds] is *more* sinful and displeasing to God," such good works at least are *less displeasing* to God. The implication here is that there is a category of moral acts performed by the unregenerate that are *more pleasing* to God than their *non*-performance would be (p. 39).

---

9. Westminster Confession of Faith, 16.7, in *Creeds of Christendom*, 635, 636.

No such implication exists. No such implication is possible. The express testimony of the article rules out the implication that Dr. Mouw likes to see in the article. The article rules out this implication decisively. Regarding those very works of the unregenerate that the defenders of common grace view as proof of common grace—works that as to their "matter" are commanded by God, works that are of "good use" to mankind—Westminster says that they are "sinful, and can not please God." When Westminster goes on to say that the neglect of these works by the unregenerated is "more sinful and displeasing unto God," it is by no means implying that the performance of these works by the unregenerated is a good work. Westminster says that the doing of these deeds is sinful and displeasing to God. But the failure to do them would be even worse sin on the part of the unregenerated. Performing these deeds displeases God; not performing these deeds displeases Him even more.

The comparison in the creed is between sinful and more sinful, not between good and bad. It is between displeasing God and displeasing God even more, not between pleasing Him and displeasing Him. There are degrees of wickedness.

When an unregenerated husband lives faithfully with his wife and cares devotedly for his children, he sins. Westminster explains why: "because [his faithfulness and care] proceed not from a heart purified by faith, nor are done in a right manner, according to the Word, nor to a right end, the glory of God." If he commits adultery and abandons his children, he sins even more greatly.

Common Grace in Arminian Theology

The confessions do not teach common grace. They do, however, mention that theory. It does not escape our attention that in their discussion of common grace, defenders of that theory never refer to the one article in the confessions that mentions common grace by name.

The true doctrine having been explained, the Synod *rejects* the errors of those who teach that the corrupt and natural man can so well use the common grace (by which they understand the light of nature), or the gifts still left him after the fall, that he can gradually gain by their good use a greater, namely, the evangelical or saving grace and salvation itself. And that in this way God on His part shows Himself ready to reveal Christ unto all men, since He applies to all sufficiently and efficiently the means necessary to conversion.[10]

The Arminians taught common grace. It is true that their purpose with it was not merely a restraint of sin in the unregenerated in order to produce a good culture. The Arminians were playing for higher stakes: man's achieving his own salvation by the use of his common grace ability for good. Nevertheless, common grace in the Arminian scheme was just what it is in the scheme of the Reformed defenders of common grace today: a weakening of total depravity; the ascription of real ability for good to the natural man; and the affirmation of a favor of God to all men without exception—a favor that then inevitably expresses itself in this, that "God on His part shows Himself ready to reveal Christ unto all men"!

The one time that the Canons mention common grace, they reject it as an error opposed to the truth of the gospel.

There is no basis for common grace in the Reformed creeds. On the contrary, the Reformed creeds condemn the theory both by name and in all its main elements.

The Reformed and Presbyterian churches worldwide may take counsel together to banish the Protestant Reformed Churches from the camp of the Reformed for their rejection of common grace. The truth is that insofar as they embrace common grace, those churches place themselves outside the

---

10. Canons of Dordt, III/IV, Rejection of Errors, 5, in "The Three Forms of Unity," Mission Committee of the Protestant Reformed Churches, repr. 1999, 64; Schaff does not include an English translation of the "Rejection of Errors" sections of the Canons.

sphere of the Reformed faith. It is the Protestant Reformed Churches and other churches repudiating common grace that are Reformed on this issue, even though they be outside the camp.

5

The Seeming Good of the Ungodly

WE COME NOW TO THE REAL REASONS WHY DR. RICH-
ard Mouw embraces the theory of a common grace of God
upon and in unregenerated humans. These reasons are evident in *He Shines in All That's Fair.* The reasons are not the
clear, abundant, powerful testimony of Holy Scripture, much
less the teaching of the Reformed confessions. The reasons
are that Dr. Mouw sees decent unbelievers performing deeds
of justice, kindness, and mercy; that Dr. Mouw finds in himself a feeling of delight at the splendid skills and a feeling of
sorrow at the dire distress of ungodly persons; and that
Dr. Mouw is convinced that he and other Christians are duty-
bound to cooperate with non-Christians on behalf of a good,
even God-glorifying, culture.

Although most defenders of common grace are not as candid as Richard Mouw, these are the real reasons for the advocacy of common grace by all its defenders.

We must not underestimate the power of these reasons, or
grounds, for the theory of common grace. What we see with
our own eyes, our own feelings especially of sympathy with the
suffering, and our natural impulse to improve the world, regardless that we must cooperate with those who deny Christ,
have a way of setting aside the confessions and blinding us to
the testimony of Scripture.

In full awareness of the power and appeal of Dr. Mouw's
real reasons for holding common grace, let us examine these
reasons.

Outward Conformity to the Law

First, there is the goodness that Dr. Mouw supposes he sees in many unregenerated men and women.

> As a Calvinist, I accept the fundamental classification of humankind into two categories, the elect and the non-elect, and I believe that while we are all totally depraved, God enables his redeemed people to perform acts of righteousness that would not be possible apart from divine grace. But I also witness—regularly, I must emphasize—acts of kindness on the part of the unredeemed that clearly seem to be in conformity to revealed standards of righteousness. Nor am I inclined simply to dismiss these acts as nothing more than well-disguised deeds of unrighteousness. There is, for example, a large moral difference between the acts of the courageous, unbelieving white people who risked and even lost their lives in the American civil rights struggle of the 1960s and the acts of those unbelievers who willfully carried out Hitler's orders in exterminating the Jews (p. 38).

It is not only the case that these deeds seem good to Dr. Mouw, but Mouw affirms that these works are good in the judgment of God. They are not as good as the works that the regenerated perform in the power of the sanctifying Spirit of Christ, but they are truly good. These deeds of the unregenerated please God. "God also gives positive *moral* appraisals to non-elect persons" (p. 37).

The error of this evaluation of the seeming goodness of natural men and women is not necessarily that it overlooks base motives in every case. Not every unbelieving husband loves his wife only for his own selfish ends. Not every ungodly soldier who throws himself on a hand grenade to save his buddies does so for posthumous fame. There is a natural love that moves the mother to sacrifice herself for her child and the soldier to give his life for his comrades. There is a natural zeal for earthly liberty that motivates the patriot to deny himself for his country. There is even a natural affection for the human race that drives some to spend their lives and fortunes for the good of mankind.

The Ignored Goodness of God

The error of the evaluation of the deeds of many unregenerated as good is not so much that it esteems the seeming good of the ungodly too much. Rather, the error is that it esteems God too little. Indeed, it esteems God not at all. For the evaluation of the seemingly good works of the ungodly as truly good, that is, good in the appraisal of God Himself, leaves out that these works *are not done to the glory of God.* The sinner does not do them in the service of God. The one who performs these deeds is not motivated by thankfulness to God for His gracious salvation in Jesus Christ.

But such is the Godhead of the triune, one, true God revealed in Jesus Christ; such is His weightiness, His worth, and His goodness with regard to us human creatures and our works; that whatever work does not take Him into account, does not aim at and end in Him, and does not manifest and promote His glory—that work is sin. It is gross sin. Comparatively, it is far worse—*infinitely* worse—than a sin that merely fails to work for the welfare of, and thus injures, one's fellowman.

No matter that a work is full of the natural love of a mother for her child, or even that an entire life of works is unselfishly devoted to the human race and its welfare (as though the welfare of the human race were possible apart from God in Jesus Christ!), the work and the life are base and evil. They represent man seeking man, man serving man, man worshiping man, man glorifying man.

"Rather than the Creator, who is blessed for ever. Amen" (Rom. 1:25).

The fundamental truth about good works is that it is the goodness of the goal or end of a work—God Himself, who alone is good (Matt. 19:17)—that makes a work good. No more than a rifle-shot can be good that misses the target—because the rifleman deliberately and foolishly aimed elsewhere, regardless that the shot in other respects shows some remarkable features, for example, that the eye of the rifleman was accurate, the aim was steady, and the bullet hit the target that was sighted—can a work be good that ignores God. Of course, if a work ignores God, it insults and opposes Him.

The fundamental truth about good works is God. God and His glory as the end, or aim, or goal of a work constitute the goodness of a work. For God to appraise a work as good that is not directed to God and His glory would be for God to deny Himself.

Evaluation of Works in the Reformed Tradition

This God-centered estimation of all the works of men is prominent in the Reformed tradition. In John Calvin's book on the very subject of the total depravity of the natural man, that is, man apart from the regenerating grace of God in Jesus Christ, *The Bondage and Liberation of the Will,* he wrote: "The worth of good works depends not on the act itself but on perfect love for God so that a work will not be right and pure unless it proceeds from a perfect love for God."[1]

Jonathan Edwards was of the same mind: "And therefore certainly, unless we will be atheists, we must allow that true virtue does primarily and most essentially consist in a supreme love to God; and that where this is wanting, there can be no true virtue." Edwards continued:

> Nothing is of the nature of true virtue, in which God is not the *first* and the *last;* or which, with regard to their exercises in general have not their first foundation and source in apprehension of God's supreme dignity and glory, and in answerable esteem and love of him, and have not respect to God as the supreme end.[2]

---

1. (Grand Rapids, Mich.: Baker Book House, 1996), 27.

2. "The Nature of True Virtue," in *The Works of Jonathan Edwards,* vol. 1, ed. Edward Hickman (Carlisle, Penn.: Banner of Truth Trust, 1974), 126, 127.

The Reformed creeds have made this right judgment of all human works binding upon all Reformed churches and Christians. The Westminster Confession of Faith judges all works done by unregenerate persons to be sinful. Specifically, Westminster judges those very deeds of unregenerated persons that Dr. Mouw and all other defenders of common grace esteem as good to be sinful, and only sinful. The confession judges these deeds to be sinful *because they are not done "to a right end, the glory of God."*

> Works done by unregenerate men, although for the matter of them they may be things which God commands, and of good use both to themselves and others; yet because they proceed not from a heart purified by faith, nor are done in a right manner, according to the Word, nor to a right end, the glory of God; they are therefore sinful, and can not please God, or make a man meet to receive grace from God. And yet their neglect of them is more sinful and displeasing unto God.[3]

There is, indeed, a distinction between two kinds of works performed by unbelievers. But it is not a distinction between works that are good and works that are sinful, works that please God and works that displease God. Rather, it is the distinction between works that are sinful and works that are more sinful, works that displease Him and works that displease Him more.

Because God is glorified only by works that conform to His law, which is the command "Love Jehovah your God with all your heart, soul, mind, and strength," only those human works that are done in obedience to the law please God. No work that is completely lacking in love for God can be good. Because the only source of goodness for fallen man is the crucified and risen Jesus Christ by His Spirit, only those works that proceed from a true faith in Christ are good. Even these works must be purified by the blood of Jesus to be pleasing to God.

---

3. Westminster Confession of Faith, 16.7, in *Creeds of Christendom*, 635, 636.

Question and Answer 91 of the Heidelberg Catechism also pass judgment upon all the works of all unconverted men and women, that they are evil. The catechism adds the warning, that we not allow our imagination to decide the goodness of works.

> Q. But what are good works?
> A. Those only which are done from true faith, according to the law of God, for his glory; and not such as rest on our own opinion or the commandments of men.[4]

God's Evaluation of Works in His Word

Scripture's judgment of the works of the unregenerated is radically different from that of Dr. Mouw and all defenders of common grace. The fundamental wickedness of the unregenerated Gentiles is that "when they knew God, they glorified him not as God, neither were thankful" (Rom. 1:21). Dr. Mouw and the other defenders of common grace certainly must acknowledge that, whatever else one might want to say about certain works of the unregenerated, they are not performed in order to glorify God, or out of thankfulness to God. But Scripture declares that for this reason alone, because unregenerated people do not glorify God and because they are not thankful, such people and all their works are foul. Upon them falls the wrath of God (Rom. 1:18).

Scripture passes the same judgment upon all the works of unbelievers when it says that "whatsoever is not of faith is sin" (Rom. 14:23). Granted, the reference is primarily to the works of believers which, in spite of the faith of the believers, do not arise from their faith. For this very reason, the argument against the works of the unbeliever is a strong one. First, the Word of God clearly makes an all-comprehensive judg-

---

4. In *Creeds of Christendom*, 339, 340.

ment concerning human works: "Whatsoever is not of [Greek: 'out of'] faith is sin." Did the civil rights activists in the 1960s conduct their campaign "out of faith"? If not, their deeds were sin. (If the civil rights activists engaged in revolution against the authority of the state—civil disobedience—it is certain that they did not act from faith.) Does the decent family man next door love his wife and children out of faith in Christ? If not, his natural affection is sin, although his failing to be faithful would be greater sin. As Article 16.7 in the Westminster Confession shrewdly adds, works done by unregenerated men are sinful even though these works may be "of good use both to themselves and others."

Second, the force of Romans 14:23 is this: If even the works of regenerated believers that do not proceed from faith are sin, how much more the works of those who have no faith. This settles the question whether God takes delight in the prowess of the unbelieving athlete. Mouw mentions the putting ability of Tiger Woods.

> Let me be concrete: I think God takes delight in Benjamin Franklin's wit and in Tiger Woods' putts and in some well-crafted narrative paragraphs in a Salman Rushdie novel, even if these accomplishments are in fact achieved by non-Christian people (p. 36).

My first reaction was regret that Dr. Mouw had not made a stronger case for his position by referring to real athletic ability, for example, hitting the ninety-mile-an-hour fastball or sinking the fifteen-foot hook shot. But the answer will be the same. The athletic skills of the ungodly as they are actually put to use, God detests. They are the skills of one who is ungodly in all his abilities and activities. They are of no use to God or man. They desecrate His Sabbath. They are part of the insane worship of the sports hero who holds millions in thrall. Honing these skills is the waste not only of time but of an entire life. God takes no pleasure in the legs of a man (Ps. 147:10). The plowing of the wicked, much more the putting, is sin (Prov. 21:4).

Judging as God Judges

Dr. Mouw has never seen an unbeliever who is good. He sees many who are decent, law-abiding, considerate, and friendly. But none glorifies God or is thankful to God. None, therefore, is fair, shining with the beauty of the holy God. All are foul. Upon them all is the curse of God, if they do not repent of all their sins, the seemingly good as well as the obviously vile. With the gospel of Scripture, Dr. Mouw must make this judgment upon all unbelievers, as must we all.

Neither has Dr. Mouw ever seen one good work performed by an unregenerated person. He sees many works that are outwardly impressive. Some even glitter. But none originates in the risen Jesus Christ by a living faith in Him; none is in accordance with the will of God that a man love Him from the heart; and none aims higher than the earth and the human race.

Not one work of the unregenerated man or woman, therefore, is fair. God's own beauty does not shine in any of the works of the ungodly. All the works of unbelievers are foul with the depravity of seeking man rather than God. Upon these works falls the wrath of God, now and in the final judgment. Dr. Mouw is called to make this searing, humbling judgment of the gospel, upon all the works of man apart from Christ, his own, as are we all.

God shines in all that's fair. What is fair is that in nature which still shows the power and divinity of its Creator and that in the human race which now displays the lovely beginning of the new creation in Jesus Christ by His Spirit.

Foul is all that which does not glorify the God and Father of Jesus Christ. In and upon it all is the curse.

We will see this if we look at man and the world in the light of God.

41

6

Empathy for the Non-Elect

———•·•·•———

As seen in chapter 5, the first reason why Dr. Richard Mouw embraces common grace is the seeming good of the ungodly. The second reason why he embraces common grace is his own "empathy" with the ungodly. Empathy is one's entering into the feelings of another so as to share those feelings. Dr. Mouw rejoices with the wicked in their prosperity. He sorrows with unbelievers in their suffering. This proves the common grace of God, Dr. Mouw argues, since God must feel toward the wicked as Dr. Mouw feels. If Dr. Mouw shares the joy of an unbelieving husband and wife who reconcile after separation, God must rejoice with them as well. If Dr. Mouw sympathizes with the Muslim woman who is raped by soldiers and whose baby is murdered before her eyes, God must grieve with her as well. But such empathy on the part of God can only be due to a gracious attitude of God toward the ungodly, which, of course, is a fundamental teaching of common grace.

God's "Empathy" for the Ungodly

Mouw advances this ground for common grace in a section of *He Shines in All That's Fair* headed, "Divine Empathy" (pp. 39–42).

> I want now to frame the issues [of common grace] in terms of divine *empathy*. Is it plausible for us to think that there are times when God looks favorably upon the non-elect in this sense: that he has empathy for their very real experiences of joy and sadness, just as he certainly does for those of the elect?

He imagines a non-Christian couple who are reconciled after the wounding of their marriage by the husband's adultery. The Christian therapist who has helped in the reconciliation sheds tears of happiness over the restoration of the marriage. Mouw proposes that "the Lord himself was involved in the joy of this reconciliation" (p. 41).

Similarly, according to the champion of common grace, God sorrows with the suffering unbeliever. To prove this contention, Mouw relates a revolting incident from real life. After soldiers raped her as part of an "ethnic cleansing" campaign in Eastern Europe, the Muslim woman pleaded for her life on behalf of her baby, whereupon one of the soldiers cut off the head of the child and placed it on the mother's breast. Mouw's response, like that of every Christian, is anger and sorrow. From his own sorrow, Mouw infers the sorrow of God at the suffering of the Muslim woman. In a rhetorical question, Mouw affirms that "the heart of God also break[s] when something like this happens" (p. 42).

Dr. Mouw's conclusion is blunt and clear: "There is a divine empathy that is evoked when a non-Christian woman is brutally raped, or when marital reconciliation takes place between two thoroughgoing secularists" (p. 49). And behind this divine empathy is the common grace of God.

This argument for common grace is undoubtedly widespread and powerful. It need not be thought through in carefully reasoned propositions. It is simply *felt*. "I grieve with the terrible suffering of ungodly men, women, and children, and God must grieve, too."

Is Our Attitude God's?

This argument is, as they say, a stretch. It is by no means apparent that Richard Mouw may infer God's attitude toward the ungodly from Richard Mouw's attitude toward the ungodly.

For one thing, Richard Mouw's attitude may be wrong,

even sinful. This was the case regarding the attitude of King Jehoshaphat toward King Ahab of Israel. Jehoshaphat loved Ahab and empathized with Ahab's zeal to make war with Syria. The prophet of God sharply rebuked Jehoshaphat for his attitude toward the idolatrous king of Israel: "Shouldest thou help the ungodly, and love them that hate the LORD? therefore is wrath upon thee from before the LORD" (2 Chron. 19:2).

For another thing, certain attitudes toward events and toward our neighbors are proper for us human beings, but are not at all the attitudes of God toward these same events and persons. Jeremiah lamented the destruction of Jerusalem with all its misery for raped women, murdered children, and tortured men, but it was the LORD who did all this in His righteous anger. The prophet expressly says that God did not pity (Lam. 2:2). Eli warned his wicked sons with a father's loving desire that they not perish but repent and be saved. The attitude of God toward Eli's sons, however, was hatred that willed and accomplished their destruction (1 Sam. 2:22–25).

One instance of a radical difference of attitude between God and us toward one and the same person will commend itself to defenders of common grace like Richard Mouw. Such defenders of common grace, following Abraham Kuyper, hold both a grace of God toward the reprobate ungodly as regards temporal life and a qualitatively different kind of grace toward the elect as regards salvation. Mouw confesses predestination, election and reprobation, as taught by the Canons of Dordt. He distinguishes God's common grace favor from His electing and saving grace.

The instance of two different attitudes is this. A Christian father with a wayward child will grieve over the child's unbelief and disobedience. All his life, the father will warn the child and pray for him. If the child dies evidently outside of Christ, the father's heart will be broken. This sorrow arises from the father's love for his child, a love that vehemently desires the child's salvation. And this sorrow with its source in love is right, although it must always finally be qualified by submission to the will of God.

But no one may conclude from the attitude and feelings of the father that God's attitude toward the child is the same as that of the father. Assuming that the child is a reprobate, an Esau, Dr. Mouw will readily grant that God's attitude toward the child is an attitude of hatred according to which God in His just judgment passed the child by with the grace of election from eternity and withheld the grace of salvation from the child in time.[1] The father loves the child, desiring his salvation; God hates the child, purposing his damnation.

In the matter of attitudes and feelings toward human beings, we may not draw a line from the attitude of the Christian toward his neighbors to the attitude of God toward these same persons. The Christian is related to other humans by the strong ties of mutual flesh and blood. Out of this shared humanity wells up empathy. In addition, the Christian is called to love the fellow humans whom God puts near him, as neighbors, by seeking their good. God's relation to these same humans, however, is not that of neighbor. It is the relation of Creator and creature. As regards the relationship between God and sinful men and women outside of Jesus Christ, it is that of the awful, holy, just Judge, and guilty, foul creatures. Scripture reveals that God shines in all that's fair. It also reveals that He curses all that's foul.

Ungodly Joy

Does God rejoice with the ungodly in their prosperity?

Psalm 73 is God's own answer to this question. As regards the "prosperity of the wicked" (v. 3), by His giving the wicked many good things and in their enjoyment of a comfortable earthly life, God sets them "in slippery places." He casts them "down into destruction," so that they are "brought into desolation, as in a moment! they are utterly consumed with terrors" (vv. 18, 19). No empathy of shared joy here!

---

1. Canons of Dordt, I, 15, in *Creeds of Christendom*, 584.

God has no joy in the pleasures of the ungodly. He has no joy in their life at all. Their life angers Him, for they live apart from Him, and in enmity against Him. All their pleasures are sinful pleasures, for whether they eat or drink, work or play, marry or divorce, they do nothing to the glory of God. What joy can God have in sin?

God has no "feeling" of delight in the things that most please and gladden the ungodly. As far as He is concerned, *they* have no business rejoicing in those things. "Thus saith the LORD, Let not the wise man glory in his wisdom, neither let the mighty man glory in his might, let not the rich man glory in his riches: But let him that glorieth glory in this, that he understandeth and knoweth me, that I am the LORD which exercise lovingkindness, judgment, and righteousness, in the earth: for in these things I delight, saith the LORD" (Jer. 9:23, 24).

God has no joy in the reconciling of two unbelievers, for their reconciliation dares to propose peace apart from God in Jesus Christ. God has no joy in the "repentance" of one whose repentance does not include, indeed is not rooted in, sorrow of heart that he has sinned against the good God. God has no joy in a non-Christian's forgiveness of her adulterer husband, for she "forgives" without any reference to the sole ground and source of forgiveness, namely, the grace of God in the atonement of the cross. God has no joy in the loving marriage of two secularists, for they do not thankfully receive the great good of marriage from God its maker, nor live in it according to His will, nor devote it to His praise.

We opponents of common grace have this against the theory, that it is a spiritual soporific to the ungodly in their decent, comfortable, pleasurable, brief lives in the world. It is as if the preachers of common grace run along the banks of the lovely river on which the ungodly are drifting—ever more swiftly!—in their fine vessels, enjoying themselves to the fullest, with the preachers shouting to the ungodly, "God loves you! He rejoices in your joy of floating comfortably down the river! He has a gracious purpose with your blessed river cruise!" And around the next bend are the dreadful falls that will plunge these ungodly into eternal perdition.

I wonder whether, since the defenders of common grace would not listen to the testimony of the Protestant Reformed Churches, God will not have the damned convince them of the error of common grace. On the day of judgment, before the condemned depart to their place, they will turn to those who taught and defended common grace, and say, "Why did you go out of your way to leave the impression with us that all was well with us in the favor of God? Why did you not warn us, sharply and incessantly, that God's wrath lay on our prosperity, that He was angry with our joy, and that His curse was in our house so long as we remained unconverted to Him, to whom all life ought to have been lived? Why did you Calvinists not teach us what your own Heidelberg Catechism plainly asserts in Lord's Day 50, namely, that God's good gifts are one thing and His blessing quite another, that people can have the gifts without the blessing, and that the gifts without the blessing do not profit?"

Ungodly Sorrow

God does not empathize with the joys of the ungodly. Nor does He sympathize with the suffering of the wicked. Dr. Mouw is deeply grieved at the suffering of the Muslim woman to whose rape is added the misery of the cruel murder of her baby. Understandably and rightly so!

Who has not groaned over the anguish of his fellow humans in this world of unspeakable woe? I suppose that everyone has burned into his soul a particular incident of heartrending distress. For Dr. Mouw, it is the event involving the Muslim woman. For me, it is an incident described in William Shirer's *The Rise and Fall of the Third Reich*. There is the great hole containing the bodies of many Jews already machine-gunned by the S.S. In the new batch of Jews lined up at the edge of the pit is a little Jewish boy, about ten years old. As the Nazis wait, cold, callous, even enjoying what they are about to do, cigarettes dangling out of their mouths, the little boy, not comprehending, but fearful, clings to his father. Looking down on his son's anxious but trusting face, the helpless father tries to comfort his child. In a moment father and son will go down into the huge grave, atop the mass of dead bodies, to be shot.

It breaks our hearts.

But the suffering of the reprobate wicked outside of Jesus Christ does not break the heart of God. God Himself inflicts their suffering by His almighty power of providence as punishment for their sins. The human agents of the cruelties, the soldiers in Eastern Europe engaged in "racial cleansing" and the Nazis bent on genocide, are responsible, and they alone. God holds them responsible and will punish them for their brutalities, if they do not repent. Let these rapists, murderers of babies, and slaughterers of old men and little boys be damned! But in His sovereignty God acts through these despicable murderers and evildoers to punish the ungodly in righteousness.

The evils that anger and grieve Dr. Mouw—and me—as dastardly deeds of men are also aspects of the death that God pronounced and now visits upon a human race that rebelled against Him and fell away from Him (Gen. 2:17; Rom. 6:23). As such, these deeds must elicit from Dr. Mouw—and all of us—the response of awe before the God who is terrible in His justice and of a living sense of the greatness of our sin that it should deserve such punishments as these.

The very deeds that outrage and sadden Dr. Mouw and me—rape of a woman and the murder of a baby whose severed head is then cruelly laid on the mother's breast—are deeds that Scripture says are done to the ungodly by God. So far is it from being true that God sorrows over these sufferings of the wicked that, on the contrary, God Himself brings them upon the wicked. Isaiah 13 prophesies that the Babylonians will be thrust through with the swords of the Medes. The Babylonian children "shall be dashed to pieces before their eyes; their houses shall be spoiled, and their wives ravished" (v. 16). It is Jehovah God who will bring all these evils upon Babylon: "I will punish the world for their evil, and the wicked for their iniquity; and I will cause the arrogancy of the proud to cease, and will lay low the haughtiness of the terrible" (v. 11).

In fact, God brought these same atrocities upon His own people. When the Babylonians destroyed Jerusalem, young and old lay slain in the streets, maids were ravished, princes were hung up by their hands, and mothers boiled their own children. In all of this, "the LORD hath done that which he had devised; he hath fulfilled his word that he had commanded in the days of old: he hath thrown down, and hath not pitied" (Lam. 2:17).

Divine "Empathy" and Hell

If now the defender of common grace objects that a God who does not sorrow with the sufferings of the ungodly, but rather inflicts these sufferings, is not the loving God of the gospel, I respond, "What about everlasting hell?" Will not the loving God of the gospel punish all reprobate ungodly men and women with the torment of hell? Will not that suffering be far worse than the horrors endured by the Muslim woman or by the Jewish father and his son? Certainly there will be no everlasting breaking of the heart of God over that most dreadful of all suffering.

We opponents of common grace have this against the theory, that it obliterates the wrath of God in history. Let some catastrophe befall the world, causing misery to the children of men, and common grace immediately cries out, "Oh, God is so sad at what has happened! God is suffering right along with the stricken people. Let's get up a committee to help with the relief!" Common grace finds it hard to say, "The wrath of God is falling upon an ungodly world of unbelieving and disobedient people, who have now almost filled the cup of iniquity! Flee for refuge to the cross of Christ!"

Obliterating the reality of the wrath of God in history, common grace has a hard time with the wrath of God in eternity.

Would not the move in the coming eternity from common grace to undiluted wrath signal a change in God? Would not the absence of His common grace in the coming eternity mean the loss of one of His precious virtues? Must not a God who empathizes with suffering idolaters, so that His heart breaks over their suffering, necessarily abolish, or empty, hell? And can God sympathize with men and women—truly suffer with them—apart from the incarnation and cross of Jesus Christ? Hebrews 4:15 connects the sympathy of the Son of God with the high priesthood of Jesus: "For we have not an high priest which cannot be touched with the feeling of our infirmities; but was in all points tempted like as we are, yet without sin."

It is vital that we proclaim, "He shines in all that's fair."

Everything is at stake in confessing also, "and curses all that's foul."

7

Culture, Mainly Culture

———— •┄•┄• ————

Common Grace for Culture

WHEREVER COMMON GRACE IS DEFENDED, THE MAIN reason is "culture." Its defenders believe that common grace is necessary to account for culture. Common grace is necessary to explain the political, scientific, technological, medical, and artistic developments of the world of the ungodly. Common grace is necessary to justify a Christian's use of the cultural products of the ungodly world. Common grace is necessary as the power and warrant of the Christian's earthly life in the world.

Culture was the driving force behind Abraham Kuyper's (and Herman Bavinck's) elaborate development of and strong emphasis on common grace. In his *Lectures on Calvinism,* Kuyper made common grace fundamental to the believer's relation to the world.

> The third fundamental relation which decides the interpretation of life is the relation which you bear *to the world.* As previously stated, there are three principal elements with which you come into touch: viz., God, man and the world. The relation to God and to man into which Calvinism places you being thus reviewed, the third and last fundamental relation is in order: viz., your attitude *toward the world* . . . In this also . . . [Calvinism] has . . . honored . . . *the world* as a Divine creation, and has at once placed to the front the great principle that there is a *particular grace* which works Salvation, and also a *common grace* by which God, maintaining the life

51

of the world, relaxes the curse which rests upon it, arrests its process of corruption, and thus allows the untrammeled development of our life in which to glorify Himself as Creator.[1]

Kuyper scored opponents of his common grace theory as guilty of "turning their back on ordinary human life in spiritual one-sidedness and presumptuous pride."[2]

Similarly, Herman Bavinck presented common grace as the solution to the problem of "religion and culture." According to Bavinck, "The entirety of the rich life of nature and society exists thanks to God's common grace."[3]

Culture was at the bottom of the Christian Reformed Church's adoption of the three points of common grace in 1924. The evidence was its stinging criticism of those who objected to common grace as world-fleeing Anabaptists.

Culture is also the main ground in Dr. Richard Mouw's defense of common grace. The third, last, and most important reason why Mouw advocates common grace is culture. The subtitle of the book makes this plain: *Culture and Common Grace.*

Mouw expresses his cultural concern at the outset.

> In these pages I will reflect on the notion of "common grace," as it has been debated by thinkers in the Calvinist tradition. What is it that Christians can assume they have in common with people who have not experienced the saving grace that draws a sinner into a restored relationship with God? (p. 3).
>
> We need to search for the proper grounds of commonness. But it is important to search carefully. On what basis do we posit a commonality between those who have put their faith in Jesus Christ and those who have not done so? This question has particular importance as we try to articulate a biblical perspective for Christian involvement in public life in our contemporary context (p. 6).

---

1. Abraham Kuyper, *Lectures on Calvinism* (Grand Rapids, Mich.: Eerdmans, 1953), 28–30.

2. "Common Grace," in *Abraham Kuyper: A Centennial Reader*, ed. James D. Bratt, (Grand Rapids, Mich.: Eerdmans, 1998), 190.

3. "Common Grace," trans. Raymond C. Van Leewen, *Calvin Theological Journal* 24, no. 1 (April 1989): 56, 60.

My specific focus will be on the relevance of teachings about common grace for our understanding of *culture* in our contemporary context. Is there a non-saving grace that is at work in the broader reaches of human cultural interaction, a grace that expedites a desire on God's part to bestow certain blessings on all human beings, elect and non-elect alike—blessings that provide the basis for Christians to cooperate with, and learn from, non-Christians? (p. 14)

"Culture," an Unhelpful Term

The term "culture" is singularly unhelpful for the discussion that Mouw raises in *He Shines in All That's Fair,* as it has been singularly unhelpful in the entire controversy over common grace. Culture is not a biblical term. It does not occur in the Reformed confessions. There is no single, specific, standard understanding of the term.

The term is ambiguous. It can mean the entire, distinctive way of life of a certain people, race, or nation. Thus, we speak of Dutch culture.

The word *culture* is also used to refer to everyday earthly life in the various ordinances established by the Creator: marriage and family, labor, and civil government.

Culture often means the development, use, and enjoyment of education, art, and science. If a woman has graduated from a university, preferably an Ivy League school, reads a little Shakespeare, and attends the symphony now and then, she is popularly thought to be cultured. Closely associated with this understanding of culture is the awed use of the word by many college professors, Christians among them, to refer to "the glory that was Greece."

Although most defenders of common grace are loath to admit it, not only the Reformed tradition in the days of its strength, but also the Christian tradition in the days of its purity, consigned culture to the abyss. They had in mind the lawless, shameless way of life of a nation or a society that was well-developed in godlessness. Culture in this sense comes very close to the meaning of "world" in 1 John 2:15–17: "Love not the world, neither the things that are in the world. If any man love the world, the love of the Father is not in him. For all that is in the world, the lust of the flesh, and the lust of the eyes, and the pride of life, is not of the Father, but is of the world. And the world passeth away, and the lust thereof: but he that doeth the will of God abideth for ever."

What sometimes happens when the issue of common grace and culture is discussed and debated in these terms is that the defender of common grace speaks well of culture in one or all of the first three senses of the term as outlined above, whereas the opponent of common grace condemns culture in the fourth sense of the term. Or, as is more often the case, the opponent of common grace repudiates common grace as approving culture in the fourth sense—the wicked way of life of the ungodly world—whereupon the defenders of common grace make him out to be an anti-cultural barbarian or, what seemingly is worse, an Anabaptist, as though he rejected culture in the first three senses.

Because the term "culture" is ambiguous and unhelpful, I want to address Dr. Mouw's deepest concerns in his defense of common grace without using the term.

The Deepest Concerns of Richard Mouw

In general, Mouw's concern is what Abraham Kuyper described as the Christian's relation to the world, in distinction from his relation to God and his relation to man.

Specifically, Mouw, like Kuyper before him, has three concerns. First, we must explain the continuing existence of the earthly creation after the fall of Adam. Particularly, we must account for the existence and development of ungodly men and women, especially as regards their grand civilizations and their notable achievements in politics, science, medicine, technology, and art.

54

Second, we must account for the Christian's life in society, nation as well as neighborhood. On what ground does the Christian live earthly life to the full? More pointedly still, on what ground does he freely associate and cooperate with unbelievers in all areas of everyday earthly life? What is the basis for his working with the ungodly every day on the job? On what basis does the Christian woman cooperate with her non-Christian neighbors in a garage sale, or in a neighborhood watch against burglars and kidnappers of children? With what right do Reformed citizens participate in national life with those who are members of false churches, members of other religions, and avowed atheists, by voting in elections, by serving in the armed forces, and even by running for political office?

In short, why does not, and why *may* not, the Reformed Christian physically withdraw from ungodly society as the old Anabaptists did in Munster and the contemporary Hutterites are doing in North Dakota?

Third, we must justify the Christian's use and enjoyment of the inventions and products of the wicked. On what ground may a Christian student read, and benefit from, idolater Plato? On what ground may a Christian minister listen to, and benefit from, a lecture by a heretical theologian? On what ground may a Christian enjoy classical music written by ungodly Mozart and performed by a mostly unbelieving symphony orchestra under the direction of a worldly conductor? On what ground may Richard Mouw, when he is not hard at work writing apologies for common grace, relax by watching Tiger Woods play golf, and even take pleasure in Woods' putting ability?

Can We Live Rightly in the World without Common Grace?

In every case, the explanation is common grace, says Richard Mouw. Most Reformed and Presbyterian churches agree.

Common grace accounts for the continuing existence of the fallen earthly creation, especially the development of the ungodly world in history. Common grace is the warrant and power of the Christian's earthly life in society. Common grace justifies the Christian's use of the world's (and here I allow myself the use of the term I have banned) "cultural products."

Further, charge the champions of common grace, whoever has the audacity to deny common grace cannot explain the continuing existence of creation. Neither can the one who denies common grace account for the grand civilizations of ungodly nations with their remarkable achievements in politics, art, and science.

Most serious of all, to deny common grace is to shut oneself up to recommending that Christians withdraw as much as possible from life in society, avoiding contact with unbelievers and renouncing the music, art, literature, medicine, science, and technology of the wicked world.

At the very least, one who denies common grace has no positive, principled ground for full, active life in this world. If he must work with unbelievers in the factory or office, he tries not to talk with them. If a Christian student reads Shakespeare or A. E. Housman, he does so in secret and with a guilty conscience. If a Reformed woman attends the symphony, she skulks, hoping that no one sees her there.

The alternative to common grace, as regards this vitally important aspect of the doctrine, is Anabaptist world-flight.

It was Abraham Kuyper who first attempted to crush all opposition to his theory of common grace by this demeaning, damning indictment.

The Christian Reformed Church enthusiastically followed Kuyper's lead in its calculated campaign against the foes of common grace in 1924 and the years that followed as it drummed Herman Hoeksema out of the Christian Reformed Church and the Protestant Reformed Churches out of the realm of Reformed orthodoxy.

Richard Mouw publicly dissents from this unjust condemnation of the Protestant Reformed objection against common grace. Bless him! He declares that the Protestant

Reformed stance toward the world, which is basically that of the antithesis, is biblically, confessionally, and historically defensible. He finds puzzling on the face of it the passion "with which many of the defenders of common grace have rejected the views of Hoeksema and other critics of their position" (p. 20).

But Dr. Mouw himself does think, and argue, that common grace is the best, if not the only, explanation and ground for the Christian's involvement in (let me use the dubious term once more) culture.

In the next chapter, I will propose and explain another ground for the Christian's life in the world.

The alternatives are not common grace and world-flight.

8

Confusing Grace and Providence

---◆·◆·◆---

Confusion of Grace and Providence

IT IS A FUNDAMENTAL DOCTRINAL ERROR OF THE THE-ory of common grace, as taught by Dr. Richard Mouw, by his mentor Abraham Kuyper, and by his numerous allies in Reformed and Presbyterian churches worldwide, that it confuses grace and providence. They maintain that the existence of the world is grace; that man did not become a devil at the fall was grace; rain and sunshine are grace; Beethoven's musical ability was grace; that my decent, unbelieving neighbor does not commit the sins of the Marquis de Sade (so far as we know) is grace; and that Greece in times past and the United States in the present develop a grand civilization is grace.

Confusion of grace and providence is inexcusable for Reformed theologians and churches. The Reformed creeds plainly and sharply distinguish these two powers and works of God. The consequences of this confusion are destructive of the biblical, Reformed faith and life.

Providence, which follows upon the work of creation in the beginning, is divine power that keeps all things in existence and governs them.[1] Grace, which carries out the work of re-

---

1. Heidelberg Catechism, Q & A 27, 28; Westminster Confession of Faith, 5, in *Creeds of Christendom*, 317; 612–614.

58

demption, is divine power that blesses and saves guilty, depraved sinners.[2]

The power of providence is directed by the counsel of providence, which is the wise plan of God decreeing that and how all things will glorify Him in the day of Jesus Christ.[3] The power of grace originates in and is controlled by the counsel of predestination, which purposes the salvation of the elect church (Eph. 1:3–12).

The power of providence is all-comprehensive, extending to devils as well as to angels and including the wicked deeds of the reprobate as well as the good works of the elect.[4] The power of grace is particular, extending exclusively to the elect church in Jesus Christ.[5]

Providence serves grace. God's upholding and governing of all things accomplish the spiritual and eternal good of elect believers. In His providence, God sends evils upon the believer that work his good.[6] According to the original German of Lord's Day 10 of the Heidelberg Catechism, the providence of God makes all things "come *to us*," that is, to us who believe in Jesus Christ, from the fatherly hand of God (German: "*alles . . . von seiner vaterlichen hand* uns *zukomme*"). Providence works for the blessedness of the children of God. The Catechism is clear that providence does not intend, or effect, the blessedness of all humans without exception: "All things . . . come *to us* from His fatherly hand."

Providence *serves* grace, but providence *is not* grace. Providence itself does not deliver from sin. Providence itself does not bless. Providence itself does not accomplish anyone's true good. Providence itself does not reveal the love of God for

---

2. Heidelberg Catechism, Q & A 29–91; Westminster Confession of Faith, 7–18, in *Creeds of Christendom*, 317–340; 616–640.

3. Eph. 1:9–11; Belgic Confession of Faith, 13, in *Creeds of Christendom*, 396–398.

4. Westminster Confession of Faith, 5.4, in *Creeds of Christendom*, 613; Acts 4:23–28.

5. Rom. 8:28–Rom. 11:36; Canons of Dordt, in *Creeds of Christendom*.

6. Heidelberg Catechism, Q & A 26, in *Creeds of Christendom*, 315–316.

anyone, just as it itself does not betoken God's hatred for anyone. That is, from the fact that one exists, is marvelously gifted, and possesses great wealth, one cannot infer that he is the object of God's favor. Think of the ungodly of Psalm 73. Similarly, from the fact that one is grievously afflicted, one cannot infer that he is the object of divine wrath. Think of Job.

That providence is not grace is plain on the face of it. Mere existence is not grace for a man. Jesus said about the traitor that "it had been good for that man if he had not been born" (Matt. 26:24). Providence gives existence, and many splendid abilities, to the devil. If providence is grace, God is gracious to Satan.

Providence includes the evils in human life and history. If providence is grace, the flood was grace to those who perished in it; the brimstone and fire that fell upon Sodom and Gomorrah were grace to those cities; the Nazi regime was grace to the Jews; and the rape and murder of little girls by monstrously wicked men in a decadent society are grace to those girls and their parents.

God's providence will everlastingly uphold and govern hell and its inhabitants. Who will say that this providence will be grace to the damned?

Providence in itself is not grace even to the believing child of God. Consider the good things that fall to the believer. The well-watered land near Sodom was not blessing for Lot. The great wealth or the striking beauty that comes to a Christian may prove to be spiritually, and even physically, destructive.

Consider the evil things that befall a believer. In itself, the death of a loved one, or financial ruin, or cancer is no blessing, does not turn a man from sin, and lacks the power to draw the sufferer nearer to his God. By themselves, such evils embitter or depress. Not providence in itself, but the grace of God working with the evils in the believer's heart and mind makes the evils beneficial.

Consider the sins in the life of the child of God. These, too, are included in providence. Was David's adultery with Bathsheba grace and blessing for him? In itself? Was Peter's denial of Christ grace for the disciple? That God governed these sinful deeds for the spiritual and everlasting good of David and Peter, and indeed of the whole church, is beyond question. But it was the grace of God humbling, forgiving, and then renewing David and Peter in connection with their melancholy falls that blessed them, not the sinful deeds themselves—mere providence.

Grace is not in things; grace is in the Spirit and gospel of the crucified and risen Jesus Christ.

Things in themselves are not blessings, anymore than they are curses; blessing and curse are the living Word of God in and with and through things. God's goodness to a person—the divine favor that blesses him—is not identical with, nor determined by, a person's earthly prosperity. God's goodness to a person is identical with, and determined by, his eternal election, known by a true faith in Christ that guides a man or woman to everlasting glory, regardless of his or her physical, earthly, temporal misery and want. "Truly God is good to Israel, even to such as are of a clean heart," though the clean of heart is plagued all the day long and chastened every morning (Ps. 73).

Providence, Not Common Grace

All that Dr. Mouw attributes to common grace is, in fact, a matter of providence, and of creation, of which divine work providence is the continuation.

The continued existence of the world after man's fall, as of reprobate, ungodly humans, is providence, not grace. By His providential power, God keeps His creation in existence, now under His curse as a kingdom of Satan.[7] By His providential power, God maintains fallen man *as man,* though now displaying the image of the devil and serving the god of this world (Acts 17:24–28).

---

7. Belgic Confession of Faith, 13, in *Creeds of Christendom,* 396–398.

The notion—popular with those who confuse grace and providence—that God had to administer a dose of common grace to fallen man to prevent him from becoming a devil is utterly without biblical and creedal basis. The notion is foolish. No more than there is evolution is there devolution of the species. Creation fixed the species. Neither sin nor salvation affects this fixity. God made man *man,* and man he remains, whether saint or sinner, whether glorified in heaven or shamed in hell. Even the most ardent advocates of common grace will grant that damned men and women in hell will be humans, not devils. But the reason will not be common grace, since on the admission of the defenders of common grace themselves, common grace must cease on the day of Christ.

The *purpose* of God with the continued existence of the world, as of the reprobate, ungodly race of humans, is gracious. It is His gracious will to save an elect church from all nations and races to the praise of His glory in Jesus Christ (Eph. 1:9–12). This gracious purpose extends to the creation itself, which will share in the "glorious liberty of the children of God" (Rom. 8:21). Recognition of a gracious purpose of providence does not confuse grace and providence.

As providence explains the continuing existence of a fallen world, so also does it account for the various physical, mental, scientific, artistic, technological, and political abilities of unregenerated men and women. Likewise, providence is the power of the natural, cultural development of nations. The only nation whose development is due to grace is the one "holy nation," the church, the spiritual kingdom of Christ.

In creating man, the Creator gave him many unique, excellent gifts. Indelibly stamped on man, as man, are kingship and community. Although the fall severely weakened man's natural powers and made him a rebel-king who seeks community apart from God, providence maintains man's gifted kingship. In a mysterious way, the everywhere present and almighty power of providence arouses and compels fallen men to develop their gifts and powers, and to do so in order finally to establish a grand world-kingdom in which the race is united. This is to say, the power of the Creator that made man in the beginning now maintains him as man and impels him to behave as man.

An aspect of the aesthetic nature of man by virtue of creation is music. The fall did not strip man of appreciation and ability for music. As a power bestowed on man by His Creator, the gift of music is good. But as devoted by the totally depraved sinner away from the glory of God and away from the promotion of the kingdom of Christ to the glory of man and to the promotion of the kingdom of this world, the actual activity of composing, or playing, or singing is sin.

High among the abilities of men, as the Reformed have always recognized, is the political gift, the ability to move and rule a people and nation. Adolf Hitler had this gift. The ability itself was good, as a gift of providence. Therefore, in a way, Hitler and his propagandists were right, in spite of themselves, when they proclaimed that Hitler had been raised up by "providence" as the uniquely gifted leader of Germany. But, in fact, they lied, for they meant that God gave Hitler and his gift of ruling to Germany in His grace and as a blessing. They confused grace and providence. Would the defenders of common grace want to contend that Hitler possessed and exercised his remarkable gift of ruling by the common grace of God, whether as blessing of Hitler, of Germany, or of the world?

The deepest concerns of Richard Mouw in defending common grace, as of Abraham Kuyper before him, are the continuing existence of the world after the fall, the presence and development in the fallen human race of all kinds of splendid natural abilities, and the Christian's association with the ungodly in everyday earthly life, using and even enjoying the cultural products of the wicked.

The explanation is providence, not grace.

To confuse grace and providence is to go wrong as regards both of the outstanding works of God, creation and redemption.

The Absurdity of Common Grace

Common grace's confusion of grace and providence ends in absurdity. It has *Christianity Today* declaring, in an enthusiastic endorsement of Mouw's book, that God enjoys a baseball game. Common grace makes God "the big Dodger in the sky."[8]

Worse, the confusion of grace and providence that is common grace had Abraham Kuyper teaching that common grace will produce the Antichrist.

> At the moment of its destruction Babylon—that is, the world power which evolved from human life—will exhibit not the image of a barbarous horde nor the image of coarse bestiality but, on the contrary, a picture of the highest development of which human life is capable. It will display the most refined forms, the most magnificent unfolding of wealth and splendor, the fullest brilliance of all that makes life dazzling and glorious. From this we know that "common grace" will continue to function to the end. Only when common grace has spurred the full emergence of all the powers inherent in human life will "the man of sin" find the level terrain needed to expand this power.[9]

In its development of all the powers latent in humanity and in creation, common grace is the "basis" of the Antichrist. Common grace "leads to the most powerful manifestation of sin in history."[10]

Grace—the grace of God—is the source of the Antichrist! Antichrist and his world-kingdom, that is, the kingdom of Satan, are the fruit of the grace of God!

Reformed and Presbyterian defenders of common grace may not dismiss this absurd, if not blasphemous, notion as the personal speculation of Abraham Kuyper. For one thing,

---

8. David Neff, "Why God Enjoys Baseball," *Christianity Today* (July 8, 2002): 49–52.

9. "Common Grace," in *Abraham Kuyper: A Centennial Reader,* 179–182.

10. Ibid.

Abraham Kuyper was the father of the doctrine of common grace they embrace and defend. For another thing, they are as committed to the absurdity as was Kuyper. It is fundamental common grace teaching that common grace works the cultural development of the race in history. But this history-long development will culminate in the culturally impressive kingdom of Antichrist.

Lo, common grace produces the beast!

The worst enemy of common grace has not condemned the theory so conclusively.

In this chapter, I have addressed the first two of Dr. Mouw's deepest concerns, on account of which he thinks that common grace is a necessity. I have contended that the biblical and Reformed truth of God's providence answers the concerns of Dr. Mouw as regards the continuing existence of the world and as regards the natural gifts and powers of ungodly men and women.

It remains to take up Mouw's third concern: the warrant for the Christian's full, active life in the world, including his use and enjoyment of the knowledge and inventions of the ungodly and his association and cooperation with unbelievers in the activities of earthly society.

9

Confusing Grace and Providence, Continued

———•⋅•⋅•———

THE PRECEDING CHAPTER CONTENDED THAT THE EX-
planation of the continuing existence of creation after the fall
is the providence of God. Providence also accounts for the
splendid natural gifts of totally depraved men and women.
Fallen men and women remain human, and to their humanity belong some remains of the excellent gifts with which God
endowed man at creation.

Those who attribute the existence of the world and the natural abilities and accomplishments of the fallen race to a common grace of God confuse grace and providence.

Providence, which is an aspect of God's great work of creation (providence is His power of maintaining and governing
the world He made), is also the basis of the Christian's full, free,
but antithetical, life in earthly society. Not a common grace of
God, but the providence of God is the biblical, Reformed answer, in part, to the question of "the Christian and culture."

This question of "the Christian and culture" is the great
concern of Dr. Richard Mouw. "On what basis," Mouw asks,
"do we posit a commonality between those who have put their
faith in Jesus Christ and those who have not done so?" He con-
tinues: "This question has particular importance as we try to
articulate a biblical perspective for Christian involvement in
public life in our contemporary context" (p. 6).

As quoted before, Mouw's "specific focus" is

> the relevance of teachings about common grace for understand-
> ing of *culture* in our contemporary context. Is there a non-saving

grace that is at work in the broader reaches of human cultural interaction, a grace that expedites a desire on God's part to bestow certain blessings on all human beings, elect and non-elect alike—blessings that provide the basis for Christians to cooperate with, and learn from, non-Christians? (p. 14).

Life in the World

The basis of the Christian's earthly life in the world is God's upholding of the world that He made. The reason why the believer may breathe, eat, drink, move, work, and enjoy the tranquil twilight of the fall season is that God created this world, created it good, and now preserves it in its created goodness, though under His curse.

Common grace has nothing to do with this fundamental aspect of the Christian life in the world. The ground in 1 Tim. 4:1ff. of the apostle's vehement condemnation of an asceticism that despises material reality and preaches Christian world-flight is the goodness of this material world as created by God. The error of the heretics is that they are contemptuous, and fearful, of a world "which God hath created to be received with thanksgiving of them which believe and know the truth" (v. 3). They deny creation and providence. Abraham Kuyper, the Christian Reformed Church, and Richard Mouw would have accused them of denying common grace.

Paul taught that the Christian may live a full, earthly life in this world and may use and enjoy all the creatures, in a manner appropriate to each, because "every creature of God is good, and nothing to be refused, if it be received with thanksgiving" (1 Tim. 4:4).

Life in the Ordinances

The basis of the Christian's active involvement in the various ordinances, or spheres, of earthly life is also creation and providence. In creating the world for man in the beginning, God Himself structured human life in the world by certain "human ordinances" (1 Pet. 2:13). These include the ordinance, or institution, of marriage and the family, the ordinance of labor, and the ordinance of civil government. The fall did not efface these institutions. The providential power of God maintains them. As structures of creation, these institutions are good. The saints live their earthly lives in these ordinances and are thus busy with *culture,* because creation and providence so structure human life. Not common grace, but the providence that upholds creation explains why Christians are actively children in a family; husbands or wives in marriage; parents in their own home; farmers, businessmen, or laborers; and citizens of a nation.

Implied is the legitimacy, on the basis of creation and providence, of a Christian's energetic engagement with all aspects of God's rich creation. He may write books. She may paint pictures. He may explore the Amazon. She may discover drugs that alleviate the pain of arthritis. He may be president of a Christian college or a seminary. Communication, beauty, discovery, medicine, education—all are aspects of creation. In the course of this work, or recreation, the Christian may lawfully avail himself of the gifts, knowledge, discoveries, and inventions that divine providence has bestowed on and produced through the ungodly. All these things are simply part of the world that God gives to His children.

As regards the Christian's motivation for life in the human ordinances, it is, on the one hand, obedience to God's calling. God commands the believer to live the Christian life *in the ordinances,* not outside them in asceticism and world-flight. "Submit yourselves to every ordinance of man for the Lord's sake" (1 Pet. 2:13). Renunciation of creation and flight from ordinary human life in it are not superior holiness, but the "doctrines of devils" (1 Tim. 4:1). The reason is that God wants His holy people to show His glory in everyday, earthly life against the dark background of the ungodliness of the wicked in these same ordinances. Therefore, on the other hand, the motivation of the Christian life in the human ordinances is the desire to glorify God. But common grace has nothing to do with this aspect of the Christian's life in the world.

Life with Unbelievers

Creation and providence are also the basis for the believer's association and cooperation with unbelievers in everyday, earthly life in society. In the world, living in the ordinances of labor and civil government, the Christian must, and *may*, associate and cooperate with unbelievers in the neighborhood, at work, and in national life.

Scripture expressly approves, and requires, this association and cooperation. Forbidding the members of the Corinthian church to "company" with fornicators and other public sinners in the congregation, the apostle states that he is not forbidding them to "company" with fornicators and other public sinners "of this world," that is, the openly wicked outside the church. If he were to forbid the members of the church to associate with the wicked outside the church, the people of God would have to "go out of the world." This is both impossible and contrary to the will of God for His people (1 Cor. 5:9–13).

So far did the apostle go in permitting association with the ungodly in everyday, earthly life that he allowed for a Christian's accompanying an unbeliever to a feast at which food was served that had been sacrificed to idols (1 Cor. 10:27). The meal was social, not religious. The Christian accompanied the unbeliever to the feast in the course of doing business, much as a salesman today would play golf with an unbelieving client (rebuking him for any swearing) and take him out for dinner afterwards (where the Christian would pray before the meal).

Association and working together in everyday, earthly life are lawful on the basis of a shared creation, upheld and governed by a common providence. This is the "commonality" of Christian and non-Christian in earthly life that Dr. Mouw is after. Common grace has nothing to do with this "common-ality." Again and again, Herman Hoeksema replied to his crit-ics, "Believers and unbelievers have everything in common except grace."

Association, not Friendship

Association is not friendship. Friendship with the unbeliever is both impossible and forbidden. Friendship demands one-ness in Jesus Christ. My friend and I must have God as our God together. Whoever is an enemy of God is my enemy. This is the answer to Dr. Mouw's question about the rightness of George Whitefield's friendship with Benjamin Franklin. If Whitefield cultivated friendship with the godless Franklin, Whitefield sinned. God had no pleasure in the bonhomie of those two notables. The evangelist was prone to this sin. He also strove for friendship with John Wesley, one of the bitter-est enemies of the gospel of grace who ever blasphemed pre-destination.

Where lawful association becomes illicit friendship can hardly be defined with rules. Every Christian must see to it that his contact with the wicked in earthly life does not de-velop into forbidden and ruinous fellowship. Scripture is clear and insistent: "Be ye not unequally yoked together with unbelievers: for what fellowship hath righteousness with unrighteousness? and what communion hath light with dark-ness? And what concord hath Christ with Belial? or what part hath he that believeth with an infidel?" (2 Cor. 6:14–18).

No Cooperative Kingdom-Building

Cooperation of believer and unbeliever in everyday, earthly life is not a working together to build the kingdom of God in history. Defenders of common grace always leave the impres-sion that the cooperation of believer and unbeliever that they desire and that is supposed to be effected by common grace aims at the creation of the kingdom of Christ. In his *Lectures on Calvinism,* Kuyper spoke of the "Christianizing" of the world.

Believers cooperate with fellow believers, and *only* fellow believers, to extend the kingdom of Christ—in the true church, in good Christian schools, in various forms of witness to the Lordship of Jesus Christ. This work is powered by the grace of God in Jesus Christ. It is exactly the dreadful result of the fall into sin that the unregenerated can neither see, nor desire, nor work for Christ's kingdom.

Living by the Grace of Christ

The Christian can and may live earthly life, freely and fully, in necessary association with non-Christians, on the basis of creation and providence. But the power by which he lives earthly life is the *saving* grace of God in Jesus Christ. If there is anything about the Christian life that is clear in Scripture, it is that the Christian life is lived in the power of the Spirit of Christ. The child of God lives *all* of the Christian life by the power of the Spirit of Jesus Christ. The Christian worships God on the Lord's day by the grace of the Spirit of Christ. But he also works at his job on Monday by this same grace (Eph. 4–6; 1 Pet. 2:11–1 Pet. 5:14).

We opponents of common grace have this against the theory, that it leaves the distinct impression, if it does not expressly teach, that Christians are to live their earthly life in society—their "cultural" life—by the power of common grace. Special grace is for worship on Sunday, as for prayer and Bible study throughout the week. Common grace is for the rest of life—for life in the world. This is the inherent thrust of the theory of common grace, for common grace is proposed as the source of the union of Christian and non-Christian. The Christian then must be living by the power of this common grace.

Abraham Kuyper seems to have taught this fatal dualism. He wrote, "You find them both [common grace and particular grace] in one and the same human heart."[1] Corresponding to Christ's creation of all things as the eternal Son of God and His redemption of the elect as the Word become flesh, two graces are enjoyed by a Christian: "And thus now it is one and the same man, who enjoys God's common grace in the life of society and God's particular grace in the holy sphere."[2]

To teach that the Christian's life in the world is to be lived by any other power than the mighty grace of God in Jesus Christ that regenerated him and now sanctifies him is attempted murder of the Christian life. Nothing less.

Living the Antithesis

Since the Christian lives earthly life by the power of the grace of God in Jesus Christ, his life is in total spiritual opposition to the life of the non-Christian with whom he shares all things earthly and with whom he associates in the human ordinances. In the human ordinances, the Christian submits to the Lordship of Christ. The non-Christian is a rebel against the risen Christ. The Christian seeks the glory of God everywhere. The non-Christian seeks his own glory, or the glory of mankind. This is the antithesis: the spiritual separation and opposition between the holy church and the unholy world of wicked men, between the believer and the "infidel."

Basing the Christian's life in the world on creation and providence does full justice to the antithesis. Basing the Christian's life on a common grace of God destroys the antithesis, for now Christian and non-Christian share the favor and blessing of God, the power to do the good, and the glorious task of building God's kingdom on earth.

---

1. Kuyper, *De Gemeene Gratie,* vol. 2, 2nd ed. (Kampen: Kok, n.d.), 634; translation from the Dutch is mine.

2. Ibid., 638.

Richard Mouw does not agree with this judgment. But he is sensitive to the danger, and uneasy with the effects of the assimilation of culture by evangelicals and Calvinists.

> Dutch-American Calvinists and other evangelicals who saw themselves as living on the margins of the dominant culture a few generations ago are no longer in a position to debate *whether* to assimilate more. That dominant culture has infiltrated our lives through new technologies and social mobility to such an extent that our conversations about common grace are now perhaps better framed this way: to what degree has the commonness that we *have* embraced in the culture that we share with our non-Christian neighbors compromised our commitment to the gospel? (p. 11).

If the believer lives antithetically, if he "will live godly" in the world, fellowship with the wicked and conformity to the depraved culture will not be the problem. The problem will be persecution. The ungodly will hate the believer. They will chase him out of labor, out of society, and finally out of earthly life itself.

But the believer does not himself run out of the world. Nor do the Protestant Reformed Churches think or teach that he ought to do so.

Not because of common grace.

But because "the earth is the Lord's and the fulness thereof" (1 Cor. 10:26).

10

Common Grace and the Infra-/Supra- Debate

Infra- versus Supra-

IN A SURPRISING CHAPTER OF *He Shines in All That's Fair,* Richard J. Mouw raises the old Reformed debate over supra- and infralapsarianism. This chapter must have sent Mouw's non-Reformed readers scurrying to their theological dictionaries. Upon turning to the chapter titled "'Infra-' versus 'Supra-,'" many a Reformed reader must have wondered what this difficult and now largely forgotten controversy could possibly have to do with common grace.

The debate among Reformed theologians over infralapsarianism and supralapsarianism concerned the order of the decrees of God with regard to predestination. Specifically, the question was whether God's decree of election and reprobation preceded or followed His decree of creation and the fall. Supralapsarianism (literally "above" or "before" the fall) holds that the decree of predestination *precedes* the decree of creation and the decree of the fall. Infralapsarianism (literally "below" or "after" the fall) holds that predestination *follows* the decrees of creation and the fall.

Infra- and Common Grace

In raising this issue in connection with his defense of common grace, Dr. Mouw shows himself an astute Reformed theologian. First, he sees the necessity of grounding common grace in God's eternal counsel. Many defenders of common grace are woefully weak here. They make much of a common grace of God in history that has no source in God's eternal plan and no goal in God's everlasting purpose. Their common grace comes out of the blue on the day that Adam sinned and returns to the blue on the day that Christ comes again. It is not part of the plot of history. God's common grace appears unexpectedly after the fall of Adam as a contrived solution to the problem of sin—a *deus ex machina*. Mouw intends to correct this serious weakness of common grace theory.

Second, in the infralapsarian understanding of the order of the decrees Mouw finds the basis for his contention that God has two distinct purposes with history. For those who defend common grace, the redemption of the elect church by special grace is not the only purpose of God in the world. God also purposes that the ungodly develop a good, God-glorifying culture. This purpose God realizes by means of common grace.

Mouw is convinced that the "underlying issue at stake in the long-standing intra-Calvinist debates between 'infralapsarians' and 'supralapsarians'" is that of "multiple divine purposes" of God with history (p. 51). Supralapsarianism makes the redemption of the elect church the one purpose of God with history inasmuch as it has the decree of creation and the fall after the decree of election. Thus, every creature and all of history are subordinated to God's one purpose of redeeming and glorifying the church. Supralapsarianism has no place for another purpose of God alongside the redemption of the church. This rules out the theory of common grace.

But infralapsarianism, on Mouw's reading, although recognizing that one of God's purposes is the redemption of the church, allows for another purpose of God with history, distinct from redemption. Inasmuch as infralapsarianism puts the decree to create before the decree to elect, it suggests, if it does not require, an original purpose of God with creation that has nothing to do with redemption. This purpose, according to the defender of common grace, is the development of good culture. God carries out this purpose in history by the cultural works of the ungodly alongside His activity of redeeming the church. After the fall of Adam, He carries out this original purpose by means of common grace.

Mouw contends that by virtue of His infralapsarian decrees, God "is committed both to the election of individuals to eternal life and to a distinguishable program of providential dealings with the broader creation" (p. 68). This explains why "an infralapsarian [can] view God as taking delight in a display of athletic prowess because of ultimate purposes that stand along side of, rather than being subservient to, the goal of bringing about election and reprobation" (p. 62). Infralapsarianism means that God rejoices in the putting prowess of a Tiger Woods, if not as much as He rejoices in the redemption of the church, then certainly independently of the redemption of the church.

Mouw's discovery in the infralapsarian arrangement of the decrees of the basis for common grace's teaching that God has two distinct purposes with history is a masterstroke on the part of the Fuller theologian. If Dr. Mouw's explanation of infralapsarianism is valid, it gives strong support to the theory of common grace.

Infra- and Two Purposes of God

That God has two distinct, independent purposes with history is basic to the theory of common grace. The very reason for common grace is to empower the ungodly world's development of good culture as a purpose of God alongside His purpose of saving the church. The theory of common grace is senseless, if God does not, in Mouw's words, "pursue separate decretal programs" (p. 68).

In his groundbreaking work on common grace, Abraham Kuyper proposed the notion of God's two purposes in the history of the world.

> Therefore every view that would confine God's work to the small
> sector we might label "church life" must be set aside. There is be-
> side the great work of God in *special* grace also that totally other
> work of God in the realm of *common* grace. That work encom-
> passes the whole life of the world.[1]

God, says Kuyper, takes "delight in that high human development" in the world of the ungodly. In the course of history,
common grace will

> achieve a purpose of its own. It will not only serve to bring about
> the emergence of the human race, to bring to birth the full num-
> ber of the elect, and to arm us increasingly and more effectively
> against human suffering, but also independently to bring about
> in all its dimensions and in defiance of Satanic opposition and
> human sin the full emergence of what God had in mind when he
> planted those nuclei of higher development in our race...The
> fundamental creation ordinance given before the fall, that hu-
> mans would achieve dominion over all of nature thanks to "com-
> mon grace," is still realized *after* the fall.[2]

But the basis in God's counsel for the theory of two purposes has been lacking. This lack, Dr. Mouw claims to have
supplied in a right understanding of the infralapsarian order
of the decrees. In doing so, he has, in fact, acted on the sug-
gestion of the Dutch Reformed theologian Herman Bavinck.
Writing on the issue of supra- and infralapsarianism, Bavinck
urged that "in the doctrine of God's decree common grace
should receive a much more detailed discussion than was for-
merly the case, and should be recognized in its own rights."[3]

So far is it from being true, therefore, as one superficial reviewer has recently suggested, that the chapter in *He Shines in
All That's Fair* on infra- and supralapsarianism should be rel-
egated to an appendix, that on the contrary this is the most
important chapter in the book.

---

1. "Common Grace," in *Abraham Kuyper: A Centennial Reader,* 176–179.
2. Ibid.
3. *The Doctrine of God,* (Grand Rapids, Mich.: Eerdmans, 1951), 394.

Regardless of the truth or falsity of Mouw's use of the issue of supra- and infralapsarianism, it is significant that that knotty doctrinal debate, regarded even by many Reformed theologians as akin to the medieval discussion of how many angels can dance on the point of a needle, is today revived as important for the lively, practical matter of the Christian's view of culture and life in the world. There is something about the issue of infra- versus supra- that is of great importance for the gospel and the Christian life. The Reformed fathers were not fools when they studied and debated this issue.

Weighty Objections

Weighty objections to Mouw's analysis of infralapsarianism come to mind at once. For one thing, Abraham Kuyper, father of the theory of a culture-forming common grace, was himself a supralapsarian. Whereas, according to Mouw, Kuyper ought to have taken the position that God has one purpose with history—the redemption of the church—in fact, Kuyper taught that God has two, independent purposes.

For another thing, the Reformed confessions, which are infralapsarian, know absolutely nothing of two purposes of God with history. As comes out especially in their treatment of providence, the only purpose of God with history that the confessions know is the redemption of the church, including the perfect security of the individual believer. According to Question and Answer 27 of the Heidelberg Catechism, the one purpose of God's government of the world in history is that all things work together for the welfare of elect believers. Article 37 of the Belgic Confession teaches that the one goal of God with history is the gathering of the elect church. "When ... the number of the elect [is] complete," Christ will come again from heaven.[4]

Yet another objection to Dr. Mouw's use of infralapsarian-

---

4. In *Creeds of Christendom,* 316; 433–436.

ism is that, historically, the Reformed debate over supra- and infralapsarianism had nothing whatever to do with any independent cultural purpose of God with history. At the time of Dordt and for hundreds of years thereafter, the debate concerned the relation of the fall of man into sin to the counsel of God and the relation, in the counsel, of predestination to the fall of man. The infralapsarians had no intention of, or even interest in, establishing a cultural purpose of God with history alongside the purpose of redeeming the elect church. Both infralapsarians and supralapsarians were agreed that the one purpose of God with history, to which all creatures and the history of the world are subordinate, is His own glory in the redemption of the elect church by Jesus Christ.

Bavinck's tentative proposal around the turn of the twentieth century that the infralapsarian arrangement of the decrees be interpreted as giving independent meaning and value to the development of the creation in history was novel. And Bavinck's motivation, as he himself indicates, was to promote the theory of common grace, of which he was as enamored as Kuyper.

The discovery in infralapsarianism of a purpose of God with history distinct from, and alongside of, God's purpose with Jesus Christ as head of the elect church is not necessarily the result of new insight into the long-standing debate over the order of the decrees. It may well be the imposition of the false doctrine of common grace upon the counsel of God itself, to the diffusing and confusing of the grand purpose of God with all things, as God has revealed this purpose in His Word. Like an aggressive cancer, common grace, by this time pervasive in the history of both the world and the church, now extends the malignancy into the eternal counsel of God.

That this is indeed the case will be evident when we take note of the weightiest, indeed decisive, objection against Richard Mouw's contention, on behalf of common grace, that God has two separate purposes with history. And this will require that we clearly see the deepest intention of the issue of supra- versus infra- in the light of Scripture.

11

Common Grace and the
Purpose of History

———— •┆•┆• ————

Basic to the doctrine of common grace is the notion that God has another purpose with history besides the redemption of the church. That additional purpose is the development of culture by the world of ungodly men and women.

In support of "multiple divine purposes" with history, Richard Mouw intriguingly proposes a new understanding of the infralapsarian order of God's decrees. Infralapsarianism, which places the decree of predestination after the decree of creation, allows for, if it does not require, a purpose of God with history alongside the purpose of redemption. This is the purpose that the ungodly develop the riches and powers of creation in a culture that pleases God. After the fall, God realizes this purpose by means of common grace.

The One Purpose of God
with History

Against this proposal of an independent cultural purpose of God with history, there is a weighty objection. The objection is decisive. Jesus Christ is not behind this cultural purpose! Jesus Christ is not in this cultural purpose as it unfolds in history! Jesus Christ is not the goal of this purpose of God with creation and history!

The proposed cultural purpose, supposedly grounded in

infralapsarianism, has nothing to do with Jesus Christ. It leaves Him out. It ignores Him.

The total absence of Jesus Christ from the supposed cultural purpose of God with history is fatal to Dr. Mouw's common grace theory. God has clearly and emphatically made known in His Word that He has one eternal purpose with creation and history and that this one purpose is Jesus Christ. Ephesians 1:9–12 reveals the mystery of the will of God with regard to "all things." The mystery is His one purpose to "gather together in one all things in Christ."

Colossians 1:13–20 is even more pointed and detailed about God's purpose with all things. God's purpose with "all things" is Jesus Christ. "All things were created...for him," that is, for Jesus Christ (v. 16). The existence and history of all creatures have been subordinated to Jesus Christ and must serve Him. All things cohere in Him (v. 17). In all things, Jesus Christ is to have the preeminence (v. 18).

There is no divine purpose with creation and history alongside and independent of Jesus Christ. Nothing, absolutely nothing, is unrelated to Jesus Christ—not Tiger Woods' putts, not Hal Newhouser's fastball, not "the glory that was Greece," not the splendor of American civilization, not the falling of a sparrow from a housetop. The meaning of history is Jesus Christ.

The Christ of Colossians 1 is not simply the eternal Son of God, the second person of the blessed Trinity. Rather, He is the *Son in human nature, the child of the virgin, the man who was crucified and who now sits at the right hand of the Trinity as risen from the dead in His human body. This one* is the one purpose of God, for He is the "dear Son: in whom we have redemption through his blood, even the forgiveness of sins" (vv. 13, 14), the "firstborn from the dead" (v. 18).

First in the Counsel

The explanation of His being the one purpose of God with all things is that Jesus Christ is first in the counsel of God. Here we enter (with the caution that dreads speculation, but

with the boldness that dares to follow where revelation leads)
the mysterious, awesome, holy realm of the supra-/infra- debate. It is mysterious, awesome, and holy because this realm
is the eternal mind and will of God in their innermost, pro-
foundest secrets. There in the eternal thinking, decreeing
counsel of the all-wise God, we meet—Jesus Christ! Jesus
Christ is first. He is first, not in any temporal sequence, for
there is no time in the eternal counsel. But He is first in that
He is the one purpose of God to which all the other decrees
of God, for instance, the decree of creation and the decree of
providence, including the fall of Adam, are subordinated.
Freely, wisely, graciously, the triune God thought and willed
Jesus Christ as the object of His love, as the one with whom
He would have fellowship, as the one whom He would exalt,
as the one by whom He would redeem elect humanity, as the
one in whom He would renew the cosmos, and as the one in
whom He would glorify Himself.

This is the meaning of the teaching in Colossians 1:15, that
Jesus Christ is the "firstborn of every creature." *As decreed,* the
creature Jesus Christ opens the womb of the counsel of God
to the decree of all other creatures, they following Him and
serving Him in the counsel. In this sense, Jesus Christ is "before all things" (v. 17).

All things must know this! They must know their place!
They must know that they are not "before" Jesus Christ, or
apart from Him, but after Him and for Him. Gifted, prominent unbelievers, especially the Tiger Woods of this world,
arrogantly suppose that they are quite something in themselves, regardless of Jesus Christ. Common grace with its two-
purposes-of-God-with-history idea encourages them in this
foolishness. The biblical gospel disabuses them of this folly.

That Jesus Christ is first in the counsel of God, even before
the decree of the election of the church accompanied by the
reprobation of the others, is the teaching of Ephesians 1:4:
"he [God] hath chosen us in him [Jesus Christ] before the
foundation of the world." If we were chosen in Christ, Christ
was before us in the counsel. God chose Him first. Our election was grounded in His election.

The Foundation of Election

The truth that Jesus Christ is first in the counsel ought to have been the Reformed response to a clever attack on the Reformed faith by the Arminians at Dordt. In order to expand the extent of the atonement of Christ beyond the limits of election, the Arminians made the decree of election follow the decree of the atonement in the counsel of God. God first decreed that Christ would die for all humans without exception. He then elected unto eternal life some of those for whom Christ died. The Arminians recognized that if election unto eternal life preceded the decree of the atonement, election must control the atonement. In this case, Christ died only for the elect. If, however, the decree of the atonement preceded the decree of election, as the Arminians proposed, the death of Christ might be conceived as universal atonement. Election then limits the efficacy and application of an atonement that by God's design is for all without exception.

Placing election after the decree of the atonement freed the atonement from the restriction of election.

In defense of their arrangement of the decrees, the Arminians argued that placing the decree of the atonement before election honored Jesus Christ. This order makes Jesus Christ the foundation of election. What they meant was that God chose certain persons to salvation because Jesus died for them and because God foresaw that these persons by their free will would avail themselves of Christ's atonement.

In fact, the Arminian order of the decrees was both gross doctrinal error and grievous denial of the gospel of grace. It was doctrinal error because the death of Christ is not the cause of God's election in love. Rather, God's election in love is the source and cause of Christ's death: "But God commendeth his love toward us, in that, while we were yet sinners, Christ died for us" (Rom. 5:8). It was denial of the gospel of grace because the gospel teaches that gracious election is the cause of faith in Jesus Christ: "and as many as were ordained to eternal life believed" (Acts 13:48).

Nevertheless, the Arminians at Dordt defended their order of the decrees as an honoring of Jesus Christ. In their order, Jesus is both the *foundation* of election (inasmuch as the decree of His death precedes election as its basis) and the *executor* of election (inasmuch as Jesus Christ carries out the decree of election by bringing the elect to heaven).

In contrast, charged the Arminians, the orthodox Reformed order of the decrees viewed Jesus merely as the *executor* of election.

The Arminians had a point. In the Reformed order of the decrees, Christ did not appear until after the decree of election. Christ appeared as the appointed Mediator, who must carry out the decree of election by redeeming the elect. Christ was the *executor* of the decree of election. He was not the *foundation* of election.

The Reformed at Dordt felt the weight of the Arminian charge against the Reformed doctrine. They tried to answer the challenge of the Arminians by confessing that Christ, as the eternal Son, is the electing God. As incarnate, He is the *executor* of election; as the eternal Son, He is the *foundation* of election. Gomarus responded to the Arminian attack in the matter of the order of the decrees by asserting that "Christ in accordance with His divine nature also participated in the work of election."[1]

But this Reformed response was evasion of the Arminian argument. The question was not whether Jesus in His divine person is the electing God. The question was whether Jesus Christ *as incarnate,* as the eternal Son *in human flesh,* is the foundation of the election of the church, as well as the executor of the election of the church. The question was whether Jesus is the foundation of election by being Himself the object of the decree of election. The question was whether God chose the man Jesus Christ first, before He

---

1. G. C. Berkouwer, *Divine Election* (Grand Rapids, Mich.: Eerdmans, 1960), 143.

chose the church. The question was whether God's choice of Jesus Christ was determinative and decisive for His choice of the church.

The biblical answer is that Jesus is indeed the foundation of election *in this sense.* God has "chosen us in him" (Eph. 1:4). In electing His people, God gave them to Jesus Christ (John 6:37, 39; 17:6, 9). Predestination to salvation purposed that those elected "be conformed to the image of his Son, that he might be the firstborn among many brethren" (Rom. 8:29).

When God chose the elect, the man Jesus Christ was already there in the counsel as the very first decree of God. *In Him* were the elect chosen. *To Him* did the decree give the elect. *For Him* was the decree of election made, that He might be the firstborn among many brothers and sisters

As incarnate, Jesus was the first decree of God. God elected the head of the church first. God chose the elect only as resting upon Jesus Christ, only as members of Jesus Christ's body, only for the sake of Jesus Christ.

Jesus Christ is both the foundation and the executor of election.

Much as the Arminians at Dordt placed election after the decree of the atonement, in order to free the atonement from the restrictions of election, Dr. Mouw insists on placing election after the decree of creation and providence, in order to free creation and providence from the restrictions of election. Creation and providence must have a purpose—the development of good, even godly, culture—independent of the election of the church unto salvation. Like the Arminians at Dordt, Dr. Mouw's intention is the universalizing of grace. The Arminians wanted to make grace universal in the realm of salvation; Dr. Mouw wants to make grace universal in the realm of culture.

Against the thinking of Dr. Mouw regarding the order of the decrees stands the truth that Jesus Christ is first in the counsel of God. Jesus Christ is first as the incarnate, crucified, risen head of the church. Jesus Christ is first as the one who is decisive and determinative for all the other decrees. Not only is Jesus Christ the foundation and executor of election, He is the foundation and executor of all the counsel of God. "All things were created by him, and for him: And he is before all things, and by him all things consist. And he is the head of the body, the church: who is the beginning, the first-born from the dead; that in all things he might have the pre-eminence" (Col. 1:16–18).

Whether election is viewed as following the decree of creation and providence (infralapsarianism) or as preceding the decree of creation and providence (supralapsarianism) makes no difference. The decree of creation and providence follows and serves Jesus Christ, God's "dear Son: in whom we have redemption through his blood, even the forgiveness of sins" (Col. 1:13, 14). In history and culture, as in the realm of redemption, grace is particular, as particular as Jesus Christ, the beginning and goal of the whole counsel of God.

Where Is Christ in the Purpose of Common Grace?

The truth that Jesus Christ is first in the counsel as the one purpose of God with all things is the deepest intention of the old and perennial dispute among Reformed thinkers between supra- and infralapsarianism. Oddly, however, Reformed theologians often carried on the dispute without any reference whatever to Jesus Christ. It is striking that Jesus Christ does not figure in Richard Mouw's discussion of supra- and infralapsarianism. Mouw leaves the impression that the question is whether the salvation of the elect is the sole purpose of history, or whether the development of culture by the ungodly is also a purpose of God with history, alongside the salvation of the elect. This is not the question, or at least not the main question. The question is this: Is Jesus Christ the one purpose of God with all things in history, because He is first in the counsel of God?

Scripture's plain teaching that Christ is first in the counsel conclusively rules out the notion that God has a purpose with creation alongside His purpose of redemption in Jesus Christ. God never had an "original purpose with creation," whether grounded in infralapsarianism or anywhere else, which He carries out after the fall by common grace. The theory of "multiple divine purposes" shatters on the rock of Jesus Christ as first in the eternal counsel. Inasmuch as the idea of two distinct divine purposes of God with history is fundamental for the theory of common grace, the theory of common grace likewise shatters on the rock of Jesus Christ as the one purpose of God.

"All Things Work Together for Good"

The primacy of Christ in the counsel of God is the Protestant Reformed response to a particular criticism that Mouw makes of their theology. Mouw sharply criticizes the teaching of Herman Hoeksema, which is certainly the teaching of the Protestant Reformed Churches, that all things exist for the sake of the elect.

> This is where I find Herman Hoeksema's thought ... most puzzling. Here is a typical Hoeksema comment: "in the counsel of God all other things in heaven and on earth are designed as means to the realization of both election and reprobation, and therefore, of the glory of Christ and His church." Here is another: "All the things of the present life are but means to an eternal end." So the goal of bringing the elect and the reprobate to their eternal destinies, for Hoeksema, is *the* divine goal, and all other seemingly independent goals are really to be viewed as means to the attainment of that one goal. Thus Hoeksema is committed to a perspective in which the paths of the eagle's flight and the ocean's waves are ordained by God simply as means to the goal of bringing human beings to their foreordained destinies, and in which the divine delight in such things is necessarily connected to the role they play in fulfilling the eternal salvific decree.

Common Grace Revisited

> I find this belief no less puzzling when I extend it—as surely
> it must be extended from Hoeksema's perspective—to the ac-
> tions of non-elect human beings (p. 36).

Mouw repeats the criticism later, listing a number of events that, according to him, have nothing to do with the decree of predestination: Plato's writing of the *Republic;* Babe Ruth's hitting sixty home runs in a season; Kennedy's approval of the Bay of Pigs invasion; and the decline of the Tokyo stock exchange in 1998 (p. 61).

The criticism is itself puzzling. Hoeksema's doctrine here is the explicit teaching of the Bible. It is the teaching of Romans 8:28: "And we know that all things work together for good to them that love God, to them who are the called according to his purpose." In 1 Corinthians 3:21, the apostle assures the elect church, "All things are yours." He specifies: "Whether Paul, or Apollos, or Cephas, or the world, or life, or death, or things present, or things to come; all are yours" (v. 22). He explains: "And ye are Christ's; and Christ is God's" (v. 23).

In addition to overlooking the explicit teaching of Scripture, the criticism fails to recognize that Jesus Christ, who is first in the counsel of God, was chosen as head of the church (Col. 1:18). His election was the foundation of our election, as His body, with Him and in Him. Therefore, as all things were created for Him, they were also created for us. The providence that carries out the decree that all things are for Christ the head necessarily governs all things also for our advantage, who are His body.

We have not the slightest hesitation to confess that Plato wrote his *Republic,* Babe Ruth hit sixty home runs in one season, and the Tokyo stock exchange suffered declines in 1998, to be among other subordinate purposes that God was realizing in the service of Jesus Christ and His church and, thus, for God's glory.

Who can figure this out? Which Reformed Christian is not deeply humbled by this, as well as comforted in his miseries and encouraged in the difficulties of the way? But who dares to deny this, since to deny this is to deny that all things serve Christ? And Christ, *the* elect of God, the crucified Servant of Jehovah and the risen Lord over all, is worthy that this should be.

Once upon a time, the God of history gave remarkable proof in history that the universe exists for the sake of the chosen people of God. For an entire day, God brought the rotating earth, the moving solar system, and the wheeling galaxies to the outermost limits of space to a halt. All waited patiently, as servants, upon Joshua—typical Christ—and Israel—church of the Old Testament.

The redemption of the church of Christ—this commands the universe. Joshua had no doubt: "Sun, stand thou still upon Gibeon; and thou, Moon, in the valley of Ajalon" (Josh. 10:12–14). Neither do we doubt.

The "Cultural Mandate"

The truth of God's one purpose with history sheds light on the "cultural mandate" of Genesis 1:28: "Subdue it [the earth]: and have dominion." The mandate is not simply that Adam and Eve exercise rule over the earth. Rather, they are to have dominion *as servants of God,* so that the earthly creation develops *as the kingdom of God.*

Fallen men and women are unable to fulfill the mandate. By the admission of the advocates of common grace themselves, fallen men and women cannot fulfill the "cultural mandate" even with the help of common grace. With the help of common grace, the fallen race develops creation, not as the kingdom of God, but as the kingdom of Man and Satan. According to Abraham Kuyper, father of culture-building common grace, by the help of common grace the ungodly erect the kingdom of Antichrist in history. Not only is common grace a fiction, it is also a failure. It cannot do the job.

The only fulfillment of the "cultural mandate" is by the crucified and risen Jesus Christ, as God intended from the beginning, that is, by the first decree in His counsel. Christ begins to fulfill the mandate now by His regenerating grace in the lives of elect believers. A Johann S. Bach writes lovely music to the glory of God. A Christian writer uses words well to explain, defend, advance, and apply the truth of the gospel. A godly farmer cultivates the ground, a godly businessman conducts his business, and a godly laborer works at his otherwise menial task, as unto the Lord Christ. A covenant mother orders her home and family according to the will of Christ.

This is true culture. This is the only culture that pleases God.[2]

The perfection of the "cultural mandate" by Jesus Christ will be His renewal of all things—elect humanity out of all nations and the creation itself—by His *special* redeeming grace at His coming (Rom. 8:17–25).

Then we will see how in the vast, complicated panorama of history every creature and every motion of every creature cooperated, wittingly or unwittingly, willingly or unwillingly, in serving Christ and His church.

Until then, we believe and confess it.

Thus honoring Jesus Christ—the fulfillment of the first decree of God.

---

2. See also "Reformed Education and Culture," in David J. Engelsma, *Reformed Education: The Christian School as Demand of the Covenant.* Rev. ed. (Grand Rapids, Mich.: Reformed Free Publishing Association, 2000).

12

The Consequences of Common Grace

———•·•·•———

Summing Up

OUR OPPOSITION TO THE TEACHING OF A COMMON grace of God notwithstanding—opposition that has hardened through a careful study of his recent book—we have enthusiastically welcomed Dr. Mouw's defense of common grace, *He Shines in All That's Fair: Culture and Common Grace.*

The Christian Reformed theologian and evangelical leader renews discussion of the widely, but often uncritically, accepted doctrine of common grace. He affirms the great importance of the doctrine, not only for Reformed Christians in the Dutch tradition, but also for all Christians. He expresses the wish that others take up the discussion: "Perhaps what I have said here will revive a discussion of a topic that has received little attention in recent years on the part of mainstream Reformed theologians" (pp. 89, 90).

We endorse this wish, but not because we think that lively discussion will promote the doctrine of common grace. Rather, we are convinced that more careful scrutiny of common grace will reveal to many that the doctrine is without basis in Scripture, is contrary to the fundamentals of the Reformed faith as set forth in the confessions, and is destructive of both the faith and walk of the Reformed church.

In the course of his defense of common grace, Dr. Mouw acknowledges the opposition to common grace by Herman Hoeksema and the Protestant Reformed Churches. Mouw

91

states the Protestant Reformed objection fairly, even respect-fully. He is surprised that the Reformed community has been so passionate—one might honestly say *bitter*—in its condem-nation of the Protestant Reformed Churches for their repu-diation of common grace. Mouw understands well that the Protestant Reformed Churches are deeply concerned with maintaining the antithesis—the spiritual separation of church and world—so solidly founded on Scripture and so vital to the church's very life.

> At the heart of Herman Hoeksema's sustained critique of com-mon grace theology lies a very practical concern about the life of the church. The commonality emphasis in common grace theol-ogy, Hoeksema insists, will inevitably result in the "obliteration of the distinction between the Church and the world, light and darkness, Christ and Belial, righteousness and unrighteousness" (p. 24).

Although here and there Calvin speaks of a "peculiar grace of God" to the unregenerated wicked, in their opposition to "common grace teachings" the Protestant Reformed Churches "can legitimately claim...to be working within the general contours of Calvin's thought" (p. 18). Such a champion of common grace as Richard Mouw gently reminds the rabid de-fenders of the doctrine that denial of common grace does not, in fact, put a church or a theologian outside the pale of orthodox Calvinism.

Nevertheless, Dr. Mouw is a studied and enthusiastic advo-cate of common grace. Indeed, he desires to develop the doc-trine both as regards the theory and as regards its practice. *He Shines in All That's Fair* intends far more than only a de-fense of traditional common grace. The book urges a more expansive role for common grace than has been recognized hitherto. It calls Christians to implement common grace more aggressively than has been done in the past. Common grace must become the spiritual glue—the superglue—that holds together our fragmented and fragmenting society and world. In cooperation with the ungodly, Christians must exert themselves to see to it that common grace carries out its great work of creating a unified, decent, peaceful, and even God-glorifying and God-pleasing culture. Christians must institute and labor in "common grace ministries."

We admit to surprise at this vehement, not to say reckless, promotion of common grace. The grave threat to the churches, to evangelical and Reformed Christians, and to covenant children and young people at the present hour is the worldliness that, at the very least, is the definite risk of common grace. Mouw recognizes both the threat and the risk. Still he calls for more common grace. It seems to us that he allows his concern for the troubles of the world of ungodly men and women (which he thinks can be alleviated by vast doses of common grace) to override his concern for the perils of the blood-bought church of Jesus Christ.

In any case, *He Shines in All That's Fair* demonstrates that the theory of common grace is not content merely to hold its own, much less to occupy a relatively insignificant place in the Reformed faith and life. Common grace is bound and determined to develop, to expand, to dominate.

Starkly outlined in Richard Mouw's advocacy of common grace are the importance of the supposed divine work of common grace on the one hand, and the complete absence of any witness to this work in Scripture and the confessions on the other hand.

According to our contemporary defender of common grace, following his mentor Abraham Kuyper, the common grace of God governs the entire life of the Christian in relation to the world. Common grace delivers the ungodly from total depravity. Common grace achieves one of the two great purposes of God with history: the production of good, God-pleasing culture. Common grace binds Christians and non-Christians together in their mutual calling to build a better, God-glorifying, Christianized world.

These are not minor accomplishments. If real, they are mighty works of God in men and history worthy of clear, repeated celebration in the gospel of Scripture.

But Scripture does not teach these mighty works of common grace. The gospel does not celebrate them. *He Shines in All That's Fair* admits as much in that it offers one text, and one text only, in support of common grace and its wonders: Luke 6:35. But this text says nothing about culture on anyone's interpretation. As demonstrated in chapter 3, the text does not even teach that God is favorable to the reprobate unthankful and evil.

This is not an implied criticism of Dr. Mouw for failing to adduce more texts. It is simply the observation that Mouw himself is well aware that his enthusiasm for "culture," for the ability of those who are under the wrath of God to produce a culture that pleases God, and for the union of believers and unbelievers to work together for good culture does not derive from the Bible. For this reason, there is not one word about common grace and its highly touted achievements in any of the Reformed confessions.

Like all defenders of common grace, from Abraham Kuyper to the Christian Reformed Church, Richard Mouw confuses providence with grace. Even Calvin was guilty of this confusion on occasion. His few, incidental ascriptions of grace to the pagans were a mistaking of providence for grace. The abilities of the heathen in the arts and sciences, as also the regard for virtue by certain of the "noble pagans," which Calvin sometimes attributed to a grace of God in them, are the effects of providence. And Calvin himself on other occasions explained these abilities and this morality in terms of providence, not grace.

A Misleading Title

Mouw's error of confusing providence and grace appears glaringly already in the title of his book: *He Shines in All That's Fair.* Mouw has borrowed the title from the second stanza of the hymn, "This is My Father's World," with which we began chapter 1:

This is my Father's world: the birds their carols raise,
The morning light, the lily white, declare their Maker's praise.
This is my Father's world: He shines in all that's fair;
In the rustling grass I hear Him pass;
He speaks to me everywhere.

In the hymn, God's shining in all that's fair refers to the beauty, power, and glory of God in the inanimate and brute creation. The world of the hymn is "the music of the spheres," "rocks and trees," "skies and seas," and "rustling grass." Even though Christ is mentioned, there is nothing in the hymn about fallen mankind and their depravity. The hymn does not even notice, amid the "morning light" and the "lily white," the curse of God upon the creation subjecting the creation to the "vanity" of the "bondage of corruption" (Rom. 8:20, 21).

As is characteristic of hymns in comparison with the psalms, the hymn is superficial. To be sure, "He shines in all that's fair" in nature, but it is unrealistic and misleading to ignore that even in nature He curses all that's foul. What of storm and earthquake, of decay and death, of "nature red in tooth and claw"?

Nevertheless, there is in the creation of azure skies and white-flecked seas, of great gray mountains and gold-leafed trees, a fairness that is the shining of the Creator. What is illegitimate is the application of the shining of the Creator in a fair creation through the work of creation and providence to an alleged shining of God in the lives of guilty, totally depraved, and unregenerated sinners by a work of common grace. Rocks and trees are one thing. Fallen, spiritually dead sinners are quite another. It is one thing for God to take delight in the great sea creature's playing in the depths. It is quite another thing to declare that God takes delight in the activities of reprobate, corrupt sinners outside of Jesus Christ, who do not seek the glory of God.

God shines in the remaining splendor of His creation and in the holy life of the redeemed. The life of the ungodly is foul, and He curses it: "For the wrath of God is revealed from heaven against all ungodliness and unrighteousness of men, who hold the truth in unrighteousness" (Rom. 1:18).

From Common Grace to
Universal Saving Grace

Confusing providence and grace is a serious error. Far worse is the use of the theory of a common grace of God to introduce the doctrine of universal saving grace. History shows that this is unavoidable. The Arminians at the time of the Synod of Dordt employed common grace on behalf of their doctrine of universal, resistible saving grace.[1] Claiming to confess the Kuyperian common grace of rain and sunshine, the Christian Reformed Church in 1924 adopted the doctrine of a universal, resistible saving grace of God in the preaching of the gospel. This is the "well-meant gospel offer" of its first point of common grace. The Presbyterian John Murray likewise moves from common grace to universal saving grace in his booklet "The Free Offer of the Gospel."

Richard Mouw does the same in *He Shines in All That's Fair.* He wrote the book, as he himself tells us, to defend and promote culture-forming common grace. We find him concluding that common grace may well be universal saving grace. He ascribes common grace to the "Spirit of the reigning Lamb."

> But we also know—and this is an important message for common grace theology—that the Spirit of the reigning Lamb is indeed active in our world, not only in gathering the company of the redeemed from the tribes and nations of the earth, but also in working mysteriously to restrain sin in the lives of those who continue in their rebellion, and even in stimulating works of righteousness in surprising places. And so, while we proceed with caution, we also go about our business in hope (pp. 86, 87).

---

1. See the Canons of Dordt, III/IV, Rejection of Errors, 5, in "The Three Forms of Unity," 64.

Hope of what? Hope for whom?

It comes as no surprise then that on the last full page of the book, Dr. Mouw allows for the transformation of his—and Kuyper's—common grace into universal saving grace.

> I do want to make it clear that while I am no universalist, my own inclination is to emphasize the "wideness in God's mercy" rather than the "small number of the elect" motif that has often dominated the Calvinist outlook. I take seriously the Bible's vision of the final gathering-in of the elect, of that "great multitude that no one could count, from every nation, from all tribes and peoples and languages," who shout the victory cry, "Salvation belongs to our God who is seated on the throne, and to the Lamb" (Revelation 7:9–10). *For all I know—and for all any of us can know—much of what we now think of as common grace may in the end time be revealed to be saving grace* (p. 100; emphasis added).

It is impossible to restrict a favorable attitude of God toward men to this life. It is impossible to confine a divine power that delivers from sin and produces good works to the life of earthly culture. Such a favorable attitude and divine power—grace—demands to be viewed, and proclaimed, as saving grace—*universal* saving grace.

Christian Reformed theologian Lewis B. Smedes was both candid and perceptive when he wrote,

> There is no such thing, it seems to me now, as a second-class, or common, grace. God's grace can never be common, never second rate. It is always special. Always amazing. I now believe that the whole idea of an inferior grace for reprobates was something dreamed up to make the doctrine of reprobation seem a mite less horrible than it is. If we stop insulting God by ascribing such a dark doctrine to him, we will have no need of any "common grace." We will have only the one marvelous grace of God for all humankind. What all this comes down to is this: The most glorious thing about God is that he made us not so that we could give him glory, but that he could give us love. And that great love leads him to be gracious to all.[2]

---

2. Lewis B. Smedes, *My God and I: A Spiritual Memoir* (Grand Rapids, Mich.: Eerdmans, 2003), 118, 119.

God has only one grace for sinners, expressing the love of His being, delivering from sin and death, and blessing with goodness and life.

The doctrine of common grace taught by Abraham Kuyper, adopted by the Christian Reformed Church, and defended by Richard Mouw is, in principle, universalism. Invariably, the doctrine also manifests itself in some form of universalism, whether that of grace for all in the preaching, or that of a death of Christ for all, or that of the actual salvation of all in the end.

Whatever the form, universalism is the destruction of the Reformed faith, that is, the biblical gospel of particular, sovereign grace.

An Afterword

Two recent developments illustrate the deadly consequences of the doctrine of common grace that Richard J. Mouw defends in *He Shines in All That's Fair.* Virtually all Reformed, Presbyterian, and evangelical churches embrace, confess, and practice this doctrine. One development has to do with the Christian life. Calvin College, the college of the Christian Reformed Church in Grand Rapids, Michigan, sponsored a concert by notorious lesbians. The lesbians sang to the Calvin students of "love, romance, and relationships." Hosting the concert by the lesbians and another concert by a band that uses obscenities is part of "Calvin's mission," according to Calvin's director of student activities, by virtue of God's "common grace." The title of the article in the Calvin College student paper, *Chimes,* that reports on the concerts and on a panel discussion about the concerts is "Calvin Debates Common Grace in Music." Defending the college-sponsored concert on "love" by the lesbians, a Calvin professor argued, publicly, "God is behind what is good and what is true and what is loving."[3]

---

3. Cathy Guiles, "Calvin Debates Common Grace in Music," *Calvin College Chimes* (October 4, 2002): 3.

Common grace and therefore God Himself is crooning to Reformed college students of lesbian love. The common grace god is thus wooing and winning Reformed college students to lesbian and homosexual love. Of course, he must be allowed to do so. Who may resist God?

The other development corrupts Christian doctrine, and is worse. Writing in the *Westminster Theological Journal,* Dennis E. Johnson contends that the one speaking in Romans 7:7–25 is an unregenerated man. This unregenerated man possesses the significant spiritual ability and goodness that he claims in the passage, by virtue of God's common grace. Romans 7 "attests the way in which God, in his common grace, grants ethical insight and sensitivity even to the unregenerate." The title of Johnson's article is "Spiritual Antithesis: Common Grace, and Practical Theology."[4]

Since the man of Romans 7 claims a will that chooses the good and hates the evil, even to the point of delighting in the law of God, Johnson teaches the free will of the unregenerated man by virtue of common grace. This was exactly the doctrine of the Arminians at Dordt. Upon the exercise of the will that has been freed by common grace, then, depends the offered salvation.[5] This is the death of the Reformed system of doctrine as set down in the Canons of Dordt and the Westminster Confession of Faith.

The *Westminster Theological Journal* is the journal of Westminster Theological Seminary in Pennsylvania. Dennis E. Johnson is professor of practical theology at Westminster Theological Seminary in California.

This is where common grace brings the churches, schools, theologians, and young people who believe and practice this pernicious doctrine.

---

4. Dennis E. Johnson, "Spiritual Antithesis: Common Grace, and Practical Theology," *Westminster Theological Journal* 64, no. 1 (Spring 2002): 73–94.

5. See Canons of Dordt, III/IV, Rejection of Errors, 5, in "The Three Forms of Unity," 64, quoted in chapter 4.

Do Reformed people really want to go there?

By the one, sovereign, particular grace of God in Jesus Christ, the Protestant Reformed congregations, schools, ministers, and young people are *not* going there.